Advance Praise for

THE BEECHERS

"*The Beechers* is a reminder that history does not live only in monumental buildings and famous people, but in the family stories that we all carry with us. Steve Sierlecki's Milwaukee family story has plenty of history, as well as some great Prohibition-era drama and intrigue."

— *Bobby Tanzilo, Senior Editor/Writer for OnMilwaukee*

"Steve Sierlecki has pulled off a minor miracle with the telling of his family's story, *The Beechers*, with a keen eye for detail and word pictures that put the reader smack dab in the middle of his sweeping canvas.

While it is a very personal account, it is really the story of America in the 20th century. A country built by wave after wave of immigrants who landed here with little or nothing at all, but with their blood, sweat, and tears built the nation and their families side by side.

It is nothing short of magical how Sierlecki writes about things that happened decades before he was born as if he were narrating them as he saw them. It is a joy to read, and you may see your own family in these pages."

— *CP Christopher Peppas, journalist and freelance writer/editor*

The

BEECHERS

A Milwaukee Family Story

STEPHEN SIERLECKI

Ten|16
PRESS

www.ten16press.com - Waukesha, WI

To journeys we can never fully understand or appreciate.

In memory of Carol, Margaret, Joan, Jim, and John.

Dedicated to Marie.

"The only thing worth writing about is the
human heart in conflict with itself."
~ William Faulkner

CONTENTS

PREFACE

I grew up the third of seven children in a working-class Milwaukee family. To make ends meet, my artist father plied his talent in the employ of firms specializing in ornate interior renovation, mostly Catholic churches but also, theaters, elegant hotels and other historic structures of distinction. He may have been the most talented card-carrying member of Painters Local 781, ever. My mother was a housewife. She never worked a paying job in her life, nor did she ever drive a car. Her kids and her husband were her life. Her heart was as sweet as they come, an introvert with lightness and humor. Her mantra: *Smile, it's the best thing to wear.* They went through tough times growing up, as millions did, coming of age during the Great Depression and World War II years. Still, as my own decades passed, some of the things I learned about my maternal family history had some people telling me: you should write a book about it. Well, after forty-plus working years and a late-2015 chat with my cousin, Julie, the time was right to get started. It began as a joint project. We took stock of old photos and memorabilia, mostly drawn from boxes in storage since Julie's mother died in 2011. By mid-2016, we had met several times, sharing with each other what we knew about our grandfather, his marital life and his children, our mothers among them. When it came time to get the writing done, though, one reality became apparent. With Julie still working full-time, I would have to do it. Lucky me. I stumbled into just the right new passion to fill my sexagenarian, retiree void.

Writing my first book would not have been possible without lots of help and inspiration. Credit is due to my writing coach, Jenny Benjamin. Through her experience as an educator and award-winning poet and novelist, I developed a presentable writing style. This credit also extends to Dan Pierce, who pointed me in Jenny's direction after he co-wrote his own family memoir with her. It's titled, *How We Got Here* and you can find it on Amazon Books. Further thanks to Gary Rubin for his editing contributions and knowledge shared.

To my publisher, Shannon Ishizaki, and her TEN16 production team members, Kim Suhr, Kaeley Dunteman, and Lauren Blue. Special thanks to Martin Weirich, the second cousin I never knew existed until starting this project. Martin furnished several of the pictures contained within, taken as far back as 88 years ago by his father, Jerome Weirich Sr. Having never seen images of my mother, her parents and siblings taken prior to 1948, these pictures were the inspirational fuel behind my attempts to inhabit their characters.

Every effort was made to describe people, places and events with accuracy. To the extent this was accomplished, I am indebted to many archival resources, including the: *Milwaukee Journal/ Sentinel* online archive, Milwaukee Central Library's Frank P. Zeidler Humanities Department, Milwaukee Police Department, Wisconsin Department of Children and Families (Catholic Social Services Bureau caseworker redacted documentation), Archdiocese of Milwaukee, Department of Wisconsin Health Services – Southern Wisconsin Center, Jefferson Historical Society, Wisconsin Historical Society in Madison, works published by Milwaukee historical writers John Gurda and Bobby Tanzilo, Milwaukee Film's Oriental Theatre website, Letters of Genevieve Preiss courtesy of Jean Stangler, Newspapers.com and Ancestry. com. Ah, the magic of the internet and a credit card. If one can keep those things under control, it's a beautiful thing. A small price to pay for a wealth of ancestral nuggets and insights into life in Milwaukee from the Prohibition era to the 1960s, when the city's 13-year love affair with the Braves ended sadly.

Throughout my writing, with a few exceptions, I do not name every source specifically: the who-said-what-about-whatever. It's sort of a *do no harm* policy, like the Hippocratic Oath, but without the hippos. Yes, I incorporate a bit of humor, hopefully, just enough to give a sense of the humor I most certainly inherited from the man at the center of the story, without weakening the salt when the story's broth turns bitter.

To my daughters, Bonnie and Amy, the greatest gifts and "higher ed" teachers this life has given me.

As always, my deepest gratitude to Krys. She is a life partner, inspiration, consigliere, muse, spirit guide, proofreader, breath mint and candy mint all rolled into one.

Lastly, to Julie. Remember how our moms liked to pair us together and people thought we were twins? I hope you got a kick out of that as much as I did. Though we were born into *Beecher World* 298 days apart, we are tied in Beecher lore forever.

Me and Julie, once upon a mid-1950's time

Yes, there were times, I'm sure you knew
I thought I bit, more than I could chew
But through it all, when there was doubt
I ate pork shanks and sauerkraut
I faced it all, the whole Beech Ball
And wrote it my way.

1.

1966

S ounds that didn't belong. Rustling, sobbing. That ting of hangers clanging after a coat was pulled from the front closet. My eyes opened slowly, in the blur of that momentary journey from dream land to here-and-now. I was lying on my right side in bed, my usual wake-up position in the far-left corner of the second floor, dormer bedroom I shared with two older brothers. It was dark, except for the usual faint ray of light, courtesy of the streetlamp suspended by wires above the intersection of North 96th and West Melvina Streets on Milwaukee's far west side. I could make out the silhouettes of my two older brothers. Sitting up in their beds, they heard what I heard – someone crying downstairs. Shadows danced with a foreboding eeriness, animated by the wind-swayed streetlamp. I reached for my prized watch, that nifty, J.C. Penney, Bulova I'd gotten for my 12th birthday: 4:04 a.m. As seconds passed, lucidity turned to fear.

Then, an unmistakable sound emerged, my father, Richard, hastily scaling the staircase two steps at a time. Dual thoughts popped inside my head. *Whew, it's not an ax-toting boogeyman. Uh oh, here comes Dad.* Typically, that ominous sound meant he was charging up in an angry rush to yell at one or all of us. *Shut up! God Dammit! Knock it off!* Sometimes, the thump of his ascending steps was accompanied by the click and whirr of his belt being pulled off in a single, swashbuckling motion as he reached the center hallway leading to the open bedroom doorway, where his three eldest sons waited. *The Punisher cometh.* Time to instinctively assume a defensive, fetal position. He would come in, swinging first, asking questions later.

This time, there was no belt.

He moved purposefully to the bedside of Victor, my oldest brother, delivering a quiet but firm command. "Get up. Come with me. Now."

Victor *unhit the sack* and followed the Old Man out the room. Yep, by now, we secretly called him the Old Man, dubbed by Victor, a right of impudent passage apparently bestowed upon a first-born son. While they descended the stairs, it was now clear the sobbing I heard was real. It came from our mother, Carol. Why would she be crying at four in the morning?

Dad spoke to Victor with rushed, muffled words too distant for me to hear. I envisioned the three of them huddled within the six-by-six-foot foyer on the first floor of our modest Cape Cod house. While my ears still strained for more clues from below, my second oldest brother, Dick, a.k.a. Richard Jr., rose from his bed and stood just inside the bedroom doorway. He leaned forward, head craned right, observing the dimly lit scene below.

I heard the front door open and the sound of our parents shuffling out. They left their seven kids behind, marked by another of the Old Man's patented sounds. When he pulled the door shut with his trademark slam, the whole house knew *the master has left the building.* His door slams doubled as a mood barometer. This was his hurry slam, not the angry one.

Dick joined Vic. Equally anxious to know what was up, I jumped out of bed to follow. I was always the caboose when the big brother train rolled, ever hoping to get in on whatever their action was. My bare feet carried me down the steps with a speed normally reserved for Christmas morning. When I reached the landing, Victor had just finished saying something to Dick.

"What's going on?" I queried.

"Grandpa Beecher is dying," Victor said. "They left so Ma can say goodbye before he dies."

"What? Really? How do they know he's dying?"

"What, are you deaf?" jibed Victor. "How could you not hear the phone ring?" he added with a sideways swat across my head.

"I knew it had to be something bad," Dick said.

"A nurse called from the hospital," Victor explained. "Dad's going to call in an hour or so to let me know whether we should still go to school."

My heartbeat quickened. News of a loved one's impending death landed in the pit of my stomach for the very first time. I froze for a bit. There was nothing left to do but follow my pajama-clad brothers back upstairs.

Sleep was useless. I tossed back and forth, thinking about Grandpa. I grabbed my watch again: 4:44. My favorite number, four. Shit! Now, I was going to think *Grandpa's dead* whenever I'd see it. Heck, I was already mourning the loss of my favorite baseball player, No. 44, Henry Aaron. *Hammerin' Hank* and the rest of the Milwaukee Braves had left town for good after the 1965 season, a heartbreaking blow for me and legions of baseball fans in Wisconsin. They were scheduled to start their first season in their new home, Atlanta, the following week. My Braves had betrayed me. Now, my favorite number seemed to forsake me, yet again.

We knew Grandpa Beecher had been in Mount Sinai Hospital for a week, maybe two. My brain swirled further as I imagined where he was at that moment. Mount Sinai? What a weird name for a hospital. I was pretty sure it was the name of a place in the Bible. Sinai. It just sounded bad. Like cyanide. Just the week before, when I'd asked if I could visit him, Mom said kids weren't allowed there.

Sounded like an awful place, to me. *Maybe it's where sick, old people are sent to die.* Ma had us make get-well cards for him. I wrote mine with a red crayon on bright, yellow construction paper, nice and bright, so it would really stand out. *GET WELL SOON, GRANDPA!*

I asked, "Ma, should I sign it, Love, Steve?"

"I'm sure he'd like that," she said with an *"aw that's sweet"* expression. Geez, I didn't know it was that serious. Could he really die?

Suddenly, Victor's alarm clock went off. Startled again, I reached for my Bulova: 6:00 a.m. Victor slapped his clock to kill the alarm. Within a minute, the phone rang. He bolted from bed and hurried downstairs to answer it. Our family of nine had one phone, a beige, rotary dial set hung on a wall in the center hallway of the main floor, too distant for Dick and me to hear the few words Victor said.

Once again, Dick disappeared down the stairs. This time, I was afraid to follow and hear what Victor might have to say. Moments later, Dick came back up. When our eyes met, his face spoke before the words came out.

"He died," said Dick with a solemn nod.

Victor stayed below. Per Dad's instructions, he called around 7:00 a.m. to report the absence of the five of us who were school age from St. Margaret Mary Grade School and Pius XI High School. Two Catholic schools, naturally. Anything else was less-than. Ah, the hubris of growing up Roman Catholic.

Three hours later, my parents returned home, where their four sons and three daughters awaited. We were in the front room watching an *I Love Lucy* rerun on our Zenith console television. I heard the front doorknob turn. Ma came in first. Still crying. Dad was right behind. He stoically guided her past us, straight to their bedroom. Not a word was spoken.

His bearing had felt the same in late January when Grandpa

(Peter) Sierlecki died. Business as usual. No visible emotion. If he had affection for his father, he hid it. I don't recall Dad's father at our house, only memories of riding with Dad to his home on North Bremen Street, in a neighborhood where Polish immigrants settled before and after 1900. Dad and my brothers did chores. I followed Dad around, a bit frightened by the man we'd come to see. His place had the same stale musk I smelled at Mr. Calvy's, the old man I shoveled snow for on 92nd Street. That funk tested my gag reflex. I knew little of Grandpa Sierlecki's life then, nor did I possess the capacity to understand it even if I did. As terrible as it sounds, Dad had seemed unmoved when his father died. *Ipso facto*, so were we.

Dad's childhood was rough. I heard through his sisters about how hard their father was on his first son, stories to help me understand the roots of father-to-son hardness carried forward. Dad faced sorrow and abandonment at seven, when his mother died from tuberculosis. His father sent his five children to live in Saint Joseph's Orphanage, a Catholic-run facility on South 18th Street, its residents mostly children of Polish immigrants. When Dad's father remarried a year later, his new wife's three children came to live with him. They had a child together in 1934. Still, Dad and his siblings remained at the orphanage. Three years later the "orphans" finally returned to their father's home. On Dad's 18th birthday, his father literally threw him out of the house. Still, at age 20 and after flying his 40th air combat mission in World War II's Mediterranean theater, Dad's desire for his father's approval came through in a letter he wrote from Corsica to his sister Genevieve: *maybe Pop will finally be more proud of me now.*

At least, I admire his pop's self-determination. In 1913, at age 20, he journeyed from Telatyn, a village in the Polish voivodship of Lublin, near the Ukrainian border, to start a new life in Milwaukee. He taught himself to speak English. By contrast, when I was 20, my big trip was to Disney World in Florida, and I spoke to Mickey

Mouse. His death, 10 weeks before Grandpa Beecher's, had been my first experience of losing a family member. Indifference and the "other" grandfather.

Grandpa Beecher's death *mattered*. The pall cast over our house felt like when President Kennedy had been assassinated two and a half years earlier. Ma had cried then, too, but this was worse. Much worse.

A few minutes after Dad carried Ma past us, he emerged to address us. "Grandpa Beecher died around five-thirty. Your mother just needs some time to herself."

We were unusually quiet, having just seen our distraught mother lurch by as if she'd been shot. Dad sat with his two youngest on the couch, placing two-year old Laura on his lap, with an arm around four-year-old Monica, comforting them with cartoons and his physical presence. At some point, he took them into the bedroom to be with their mother.

Around noon, I was in the kitchen when Dad went back into the bedroom. Ma emerged, leaving the three of them behind. Her face and eyes were a matching red as she made her way to stand at her "station," facing the dual sink basins at the kitchen counter, within the area of our small kitchen where she seemed to be perpetually. Within reach, at eye level to her right, was a built-in, three-tiered corner shelf with a radio, assorted knickknacks and religious articles. Prominently displayed was a blue Virgin Mary Madonna statue on the middle shelf, a gift she'd received from my cousin, Julie. She kept a laminated prayer card next to that statue:

GOD WON'T GIVE YOU ANY MORE
THAN YOU CAN HANDLE.

On the bottom shelf, she kept a gilded-edged holy card with the image of her favorite saint, Thérèse of Lisieux. Already a nun at age 15, Therese was known as "the Little Flower of Jesus" for her commitment to living like the simple wildflowers in forests and fields, unnoticed by the greater population, yet growing and giving glory to God. A prayer accompanied Thérèse's image:

OH, LITTLE FLOWER,
SHOW YOUR POWER IN THIS HOUR.

While I sat at the table feigning interest in that morning's Milwaukee Sentinel sports section, I couldn't help peeking Ma's way. For nearly a minute, she stared blankly out the window, her eyes shifting to view her personal altar. Her welled eyes began to overflow. Her lips trembled. It was no use. Not even St. Thérèse could stop it. Ma turned to retreat again to the bedroom, covering her reddened face as tears dropped like a faucet leaking. I recall thinking that her father's death had to be the worst thing that had ever happened to her.

Grief became personalized for the first time in my life. It was a toss-up as to which thought was more disturbing: the concept of never seeing my favorite grandfather again or the unsettling sight of my saintly mother crying uncontrollably.

Her reality was well beyond the comprehension of this naïve 12-year-old. I had no idea I was witnessing a thirty-nine-year-old woman whose secret dam of past sorrows collapsed from the emotional quake triggered by the passing of the man at the center of it all. Gone was the man that she and her closest sister, Marge, referred to with a tone that conveyed both delight and derision. The man they called, the Old Boy.

Monday, April 4, 1966. It was the day my beloved grandfather, Carroll August Beecher died at age 60.

2.

MEMORIES

I loved Grandpa Beecher. He was funny, yet it wasn't so much what he said but how. His repertoire of sound effects and facial expressions were unlike anyone else I knew.

When he came to visit, he'd pull up to our house on Melvina Street in his 1960 Mercury Monterrey, a two-door, cream-colored behemoth. As all seven of his grandchildren burst out the front door to greet him, Grandpa would give a subtle wave and step toward the back of his car. He was an imposing man. He didn't take steps like a normal person but moved with a presence about him, with long, slow strides and an ever-present authoritative expression.

As he inserted a key in his trunk lock, we gathered in wonder, as if he were about to open a treasure chest on wheels. When the Mercury's sprawling trunk lid rose, it revealed a medley of delights that included several locally made goods, befitting the quintessential, mid-century Milwaukee patriarch.

His supply of grandkid spoiling edibles featured locally made Geiser's Potato Chips and Old Gold Pretzels, in the 10-cent bag size, so every one of us got our own treat. Sometimes he surprised us by substituting the salty treats with my personal favorite – a *mittful,* as he would say, of Kit Kat candy bars. Each of us got our own drink, as well – a can of Grandpa Graf's Creamy Top Root Beer. An individual can was a luxury for a bunch of kids who occasionally got to share a 26-ounce bottle of Coke, seven ways, as a weekend treat. The mustachioed grandpa logo on the Graf's root beer can actually looked like *him*. But, the centerpiece of his trunk of bounty was his seemingly endless supply of Miller High Life beer cans that came straight from the main plant on State Street, where the giant red Miller sign rotated in all its glory above the brewery. A pint bottle of Coronet VSQ Brandy was a standard pairing, always. He'd gather the consumables for that day's visit into a box and headed toward the front door. We followed him like a band of giddy Lilliputians.

Ma held the front door open, her "company's coming" red lipstick outlining the most joyful smile imaginable. He ambled into the front room, and we trailed behind with Grandma Demi bringing up the rear. Our parade ended in the kitchen, where Grandpa occupied his usual spot at the head of the table with the majesty of an exalted king preparing to hold court over his adoring descendants. We jostled for space close to him. Grandma Demi would always take the seat to his right. How to refer to her felt awkward. Both Ma and Dad clearly liked her, though neither told us what to call her. I knew she was married to Grandpa, but she was not Ma's real mother. It didn't seem right to call her Grandma and disrespectful to address her or any adult by their first name. I simply smiled and said "Hi."

Ma would automatically pull Kit Kat bars from his party-in-a-box and hand them to her father, who passed out the chocolate-wafer treat he'd taught us to love.

"Ya, hey, get your Kit Kat bar here, hey, I got Kit Kat bars here, hey," he'd call out in classic Wisconsin dialect with a singsongy flair. We'd step up one-by-one, say "thank you" and tear into our foil wrapped confection. Demi always sat in the chair to his right, cheerfully laughing as her man conducted candy bar communion.

Catholic ritual parody was a Grandpa Beecher specialty.

Like a papal acolyte, Ma would bring out the snifter style beer glass and shot glass reserved only for Grandpa B. As we savored our candy bars, our pontiff carefully assembled the standard articles of his imbibing session. He lined them up in a row – beer glass, beer can, shot glass and brandy bottle. As if performing the consecration rite of a Catholic Mass, he grabbed the can and slowly poured beer into the glass. Always the perfect pour, not quite to the brim, allowing for a crown of foam above the top, nary an over pour.

Next, he poured brandy to the top of the shot glass. His rituals were immediately followed by Ma handing him a raw egg, as if she were an altar boy or magician's assistant.

He'd crack the egg on the edge of his chalice and open it above the glass, the egg dropping with an elongated, yoke-driven plop. Legend had it that an egg in your beer was a hangover cure, though at 12, I had only a vague idea that hangover meant you'd had too much alcohol to drink. Our priest used one hand to swirl the glass on the table for several seconds, as if he were opening the bouquet of a fine wine. With exaggerated devotion, he grabbed the shot glass and slowly raised it to his lips. In the blink of an eye, he downed the brandy, his head jerking backward. After firmly putting the shot glass down on the table, he bellowed out, in Jackie Gleason style – "Woooo-Owwwwww!" We all howled with laughter; Ma included.

Finally, with a deliberate flair, he lifted his beer glass, as if he were toasting every grandkid around the table, and then raised the glass above his head, gazing at it with reverence.

Instead of uttering the sanctifying Latin phrase, *Dominus Vobiscum* (Lord be with you), our ex-policeman granddad declared, "Dominic, go frisk 'em!"

We tittered as pint-sized neophytes, in full knowledge of the sacrilegious nature of his outrageous humor. He lowered the glass to his lips, and then gulped back its entire contents before banging the glass back down on the table. He'd punctuate the ritual with a guttural sound of satisfaction – "Ahhhhhhhh." His routine always drew a mix of applause, giggles and *ewwww's* at the sight of 12-ounces of beer, plus a raw egg with yolk intact, sliding from his glass to his belly in a matter of seconds. No one made drinking look as fun as Grandpa Beecher.

Sometimes, he'd arrive for weekday visits in early afternoon while I was at school. Looking back now, perhaps it afforded private time for him to talk with Ma while my baby sisters napped, before us school-aged kids were back. I remember the homeward walk from school west on Melvina Street, and the magical sight of the big Mercury that lifted my spirits and quickened my pace.

Other times, he visited on a Saturday when Dad, whose work week often took place in distant towns, would be home. They appeared quite compatible as drinking partners. Grandpa's presence brought out Dad's lighter side, a welcome reprieve from his intense default mode. I discovered Dad could actually be deferential. He relinquished his spot at the head of the table in stride and seemed to enjoy his father-in-law's folksy verbal mashups, revealing an affable side to the man who demanded proper elocution from his children. On occasion, Grandpa and Demi stayed into the evening to watch the Jackie Gleason show with us. Grandpa's comedic style was so much like Gleason's, I wasn't sure if he copied Gleason or Gleason copied him.

Yet, my biggest connection with him was baseball. Ma said he had been a great baseball player when she was growing up. That helped me understand and appreciate why he enjoyed bringing along his ancient leather baseball mitt during spring and summertime visits. After his obligatory "shot and a beer," he headed outside to play catch in the backyard. Sometimes, it was with me and my two older brothers. But more times than not, it was just me. I loved it. I was the pitcher on our neighborhood little league team. Our first exclusive *catch time* was memorable. I couldn't wait to start firing the ball at him as hard as I could to show him what a good pitcher I was.

"Hold the phone, kiddo, hold the phone. Come here," he said. I ran to him like a bird dog.

"Any pitcher worth a damn loosens up first. Back up 'til I tell you to stop," he ordered.

After I back-pedaled about 20 feet, he extended his hand to signal. Stop.

"Always start with some soft tossing. You loosen up gradually, kid. Throw it to me nice and easy."

We tossed a dozen times. He waved me backward another 20 feet.

"Still soft, kid. Lob it to me like this."

He'd demonstrate the proper arm angle for throwing, reaching back and following through over his shoulder while striding toward me. My natural tendency was to sling the ball, sidearm style. It was awkward trying to mimic him. I didn't get it right, and he shook his head. My next throw wasn't right, either. He flashed a disapproving scowl that scared the crap out of me. Without saying a word, he gestured to show me the arm motion he expected. My third toss garnered a nod of approval, thankfully. Anything to avoid being on the receiving end of his fear-of-God glare.

He made sure I threw correctly for several minutes until he seemed satisfied that I understood. Then, he waved me further away once more, and we repeated the process. Only when he felt I had warmed up properly, did he tell me to stand at the regulation Little League pitching distance (46 feet).

"Now, show me what you got, kid."

Bear in mind that in the early 1960's, the great Warren Spahn pitched for our Milwaukee Braves. Though Spahn was in the latter stages of his Hall of Fame career, he was well on his way to becoming the winningest left-handed pitcher of all time. Batted left, threw left.

Just like I did. Using the style of my idol that I practiced countless times, I threw to Grandpa using *Spahnie's* trademark windup and high leg-kick delivery. I thought, *oh boy, won't he be impressed!*

After catching my throw, he said dismissively, "Forgot the Spahn bit, kid. Style doesn't matter. Control is what matters."

My heart sank. All my practicing to be like Spahn, for nothing.

He walked over to explain and demonstrate next to me. He reshaped my technique into a more controlled style to stay within myself. Once I finally understood to his satisfaction, we threw, and we threw, and I loved every minute.

"Stick with me, kid, and someday I'll teach you to throw a spitball and some other tricks," he said, punctuated by that devilish eyebrow wiggle he'd do.

"Spitball? Isn't that against the rules?"

"Kiddo, let me tell you. Sometimes you bend the rules. You do whatever it takes to win."

I stared back at him, surprised yet tantalized by permission to taste the forbidden fruit of rule breaking.

"You'll see, kid. The older you get."

Perched in my Milwaukee Braves cap, spring 1964

3.

THE FUNERAL

Two days later, on Wednesday, April 6, services were held for Grandpa Beecher, beginning with a visitation at Brett Funeral Home on 20th Street and Wisconsin Avenue.

We arrived 15 minutes early, the nine of us clad in Sunday clothes and packed inside Dad's Ford station wagon. As everyone piled out and headed toward the entrance, I held back. The mere thought of going in and seeing Grandpa dead made me feel sick. Dad looked around to see me frozen to the back seat.

"What the hell are you doing?"

"I feel sick to my stomach. I don't think I can go in."

He grabbed me by the jacket collar, dragging me across the seat and out of the car. As he led me by the hand, preoccupation with moving my feet fast enough to keep up made me forget the gagging feeling I'd had seconds earlier.

Once inside, I found comfort in seeing many familiar faces. With hesitation, I slowly stepped further into the huge room until I saw the open casket. There he was, appearing to be asleep, his upper body visible. I'd never seen him wearing a suit coat and tie before. Even more noticeable was the weird orange color of his face. It was the second grandfather I'd seen in a casket in less than three months. I never looked directly at him again.

Surveying the room, I saw Aunt Marge, my mother's sister. Beside her was my cousin, her daughter, Julie. Though we were born 10 months apart, our resemblance gave some the impression we were twin siblings. I sought refuge in their company while making sure my back was to the casket.

"Did you get his holy card?" Julie asked.

Still nervous, I was puzzled. I didn't get what she meant and shook my head no.

"I'll show you where they are," she said.

Julie led me to a fancy table I had passed when entering earlier, just outside the big room where everyone had gathered. She picked up a card and handed it to me. It had a picture of our grandfather in a police uniform. His birth and death dates were printed beneath.

"Pretty neat picture, huh?"

"Yeah, I guess so," I replied with hesitation.

While still trying to shake my nervousness, I wondered why I had never seen such an impressive picture of him before. Ma never talked about him being a policeman. Did he capture bad guys? Did he shoot them? Did he ever kill somebody? He must have had lots of cool stories but the only one I remembered hearing was the uniform story.

"One day, the chief came to the station house for an inspection," he recalled. "We're all standing at attention. The chief walks by, looking us all up and down. He walks back in front of me and tells me to stand on the captain's desk. 'Observe Officer Beecher,'" the chief says. "'This is how a proper officer should appear. Clean shaven, pressed uniform, boots like mirrors. From now on, I want all of you reporting for duty looking like Officer Beecher.'"

When Grandpa told that story, I imagined him standing on that desk, the model police officer. My thoughts drifted as I held his card. Why didn't I ask him what it was like? Gosh, the stories' he must have had. I turned the card over and recognized the words from the hymnals at church:

AMAZING GRACE

Amazing Grace, how sweet the sound,
That saved a wretch like me.
I once was lost but now am found,
Was blind, but now I see.

T'was Grace that taught my heart to fear.
And Grace, my fears relieved.
How precious did that Grace appear
The hour I first believed.

Through many dangers, toils and snares
I have already come;
'Tis Grace that brought me safe thus far
and Grace will lead me home.

BRETT FUNERAL HOME

Such sad words, I thought. They didn't seem to apply to Grandpa, at all.

"Can I keep this?" I asked to Julie.

"My mom gave one to me and Dan. I'm sure it's okay."

The picture was cool, but the poem bothered me. I saw my mother nearby and went to her.

"Ma, did you see his holy card? Look at that picture!"

She laughed a bit. "It's not really a holy card, hon; it's called a prayer card. That's your grandfather in his Police Chief uniform."

"I knew he was a policeman once, but I didn't know he was a chief," I said, declaring wonderment over his lofty rank, and over the words on the back of the card. "It's that song from church, but it just sounds bad, like he needed to be saved," I lamented, frowning as held the card out in front of her.

She hesitated as her smile faded. "He died. Prayer cards can be sad. Grandpa loved that song. Everyone does." She tousled my hair lovingly.

A man who worked at the funeral home announced a prayer service was about to start and asked everyone to be seated. I followed Ma to where Dad was already sitting with my three sisters. A Catholic priest came forward and led everyone in a series of prayers. I managed to avoid making eye contact with dead Grandpa until the praying ended and the funeral guy stepped to the casket. As he lowered the lid, I couldn't help but catch a last glimpse. In that moment, my childish nervousness dissolved, instantly replaced by wet eyes and a throat lump.

Everyone filed out, just like the end of Sunday Mass. Some got in cars and went their way. The rest of us got into our cars and lined up for a procession. With an official black car and the hearse leading us, we drove about a mile west to Saint Rose Church for a service. After that, everybody went a couple miles west and turned left into Calvary Cemetery on Bluemound Road. At the time, I had no idea it was the oldest Catholic cemetery in Milwaukee's Archdiocese, established 109 years earlier, in 1857.

A light rain fell as everyone stepped from their cars to follow the Milwaukee Police Honor Guard carrying the casket, faceless pallbearers slowly moving in lockstep, the dramatic scene reminiscent of President Kennedy's televised burial. They carefully positioned the shiny mahogany box on a stand above the open grave, a dismal sight framed by leafless trees and haunting gravestones looming above on a hillside. Even now, I can still hear the patter of rain drops on umbrellas, along with the faint, heart-wrenching sound of women sobbing.

With about 50 souls gathered around him, the priest stood at the head of the casket and began the Catholic Rite of Committal.

"In the name of the Father, the Son and the Holy Ghost. We gather here to commend our brother, Carroll August Beecher . . ."

Prayers for the repose of the soul. Sprinkling of holy water. As an attendant slowly lowered the coffin into the grave, the somber shrill of bagpipes began. "Amazing Grace" washed over us from the nearby hillside. Before I turned to look, I knew I would see Uncle Jim. Sure enough, there he was, in full piper regalia.

Jim was one of Grandpa Beecher's twin sons and had learned to play the pipes while stationed in Japan during his time in the Air Force. Uncle Jim was not married, a very funny man, if not a bit eccentric for a 27-year-old. He stood erect; his face puffed from continually blowing the air needed to produce the pipe's distinctive tones. This was not the silly uncle I knew. Suddenly, it felt like I was in a movie scene where the hero dies and receives a heart-rending send off. A surge of quivering lips. Handkerchiefs dabbing at tears and sniffling noses. I was feeling the most powerful moment of the day. Clearly, the feeling was mutual.

The pipes stopped. "Our burial rite for Carroll August Beecher has ended," the priest declared. "May you go in peace to love and serve the Lord in his memory."

Those words, along with the visual that accompanied them would also be indelibly etched into memory – four women, a huge tree trunk looming behind them, standing from left to right in front of the casket.

Demi was on the left, looking like Jackie Kennedy at her husband's gravesite, adorned in a black pillbox hat with meshed veil. Her posture, perfectly upright, as she stood solemn-faced in her trademark, shaded-lens glasses (photochromic lenses, the precursor to transitional lenses). She always looked classy, though at that moment, I couldn't stop myself from picturing her *va-va-voom* solo dance in a sexy sequined dress at Aunt Marge's last Christmas party. Ma said Demi had been an *exotic follies* dancer a long time ago, whatever that meant.

Next to her was my mother, sobbing uncontrollably, clutching a handkerchief to her face, more grief-stricken than anyone. I don't remember what she was wearing. I wanted to look away but couldn't. My stomach churned at the sight. My eyes slid right to escape the surge of wetness that began to cloud my vision.

I wiped my eyes and saw Aunt Joan, my mother's sister, looking placid, as always. She had a black scarf on her head and those cat-eye eye glass frames she always wore. Her expression was stoic, seemingly indifferent and out-of-place. The contrast was striking.

The fourth woman was their sister Marge, my favorite aunt, at least on my mother's side. She wore a hat. She looked wistful, yet calm, as if wanting to stay strong for daughter Julie, who stood to her left and held her hand.

Julie's eyes shifted my way. Our eyes met. I was startled, as if caught staring. To break the tension, I wiggled my eyebrows up and down, silent humor I had picked-up from the man in the box. She smiled back with a slight disapproving head tilt, as if to say, *don't make me laugh, you brat.*

It was always apparent that Ma had the greatest affection for her father. Although she appeared happy and kept her composure at the funeral parlor, her graveside outpouring was the saddest thing I had ever seen in my life. It was as if Carol Jr.'s bond with Carroll Sr. was a powerful force that transcended simply being his namesake, a depth of connection impossible for me to understand.

4.

FLASH FORWARD

~ Fifty years later ~

Julie and I returned to the place where our eyes had met on that sad day long ago. It was Sunday, April 3, 2016, one day shy of 50 years since we'd stood in Calvary Cemetery.

The exquisite naivety of childhood had slipped away years earlier. Now in our early-60s, it was mind-blowing; the world had turned for a half-century and each of us had surpassed the life span of the man whose grave we were about to visit. Like him, our lives were centered in the Milwaukee area, raising children of our own and experiencing life in what was America's eleventh largest city, once upon a time. Though we'd socialized periodically as the decades rolled by, it was the usual family stuff that brought us together most – weddings, births, birthdays, anniversaries, reunions and funerals.

Our mothers had passed on to their heavenly reward – mine, in April 1993 and Julie's in May 2011.

We began to see more of each other, both in her mother's last months of failing health and in the months and years that followed. We met periodically, exchanging stories passed down from our mothers about their family life in the 1930s and 1940s. There were amusing anecdotes about their mother and her playful superstitions – drop a spoon and company is coming soon, if your right palm itches, you'll get money soon. As for unamusing details bequeathed, it became apparent that Julie had the more forthright mum. Renewed kinship with *Jules* proffered two realities to confront: one, a realization unimaginable, so long ago – holy shit, we're the old generation now; and two – the skeletons in the maternal family closet had everything to do with the larger-than-life grandfather we remembered from childhood. Since 2011, desire to understand our family's past became a shared hobby. We'd accrued a collection of old photographs and documents in a genealogical journey that culminated in a trip back to Calvary.

On this cloudy but warm day for early April, we drove in separate cars and met outside the cemetery. Leaving her car behind on Bluemound Road, we rolled in at mid-afternoon. I thought I could find our grandfather's grave from the visual of that day in my mind's eye. While I observed the historic cemetery's 10 mile-per-hour speed limit, Julie pulled some papers from her purse.

"Here's the printout I got from the Archdiocese records office over at Holy Cross. It shows the section and row where the Clancy-Beecher plot is. It has a diagram of where each grave is located. The oldest graves are the Clancys' from the 1800s."

"Thanks, but I want to see if I can find it from memory."

"So, we're an old married couple now, huh?" she deadpanned with a subtle eye-roll that said *you won't use a map, huh, smart guy?*

"No, really, I think I can find it by memory. There was a big tree and a slope that went up the hill toward the chapel." Two minutes later, I rolled to a stop and pointed right. "I recognize this view. This is it."

We got out of the car and began shuffling about, scanning gravestones for the Beecher name. I laughed at myself after looking back at my car parked on the narrow asphalt path, concerned it could block passage. Aside from Julie, the only living souls in sight whirred by in cars on the interstate several hundred yards to the south.

"Here," Julie said, looking down at the modest gravestone at her feet. "You were right."

We stared down in silence at the flat granite marker for several seconds.

I looked up. "That's the big tree I remembered." About thirty feet away, the huge white oak had stood sentinel fifty years since we last met. I looked to my right. "That hill, Chapel Hill. I had no idea it was chock-full of dead Jesuits back then."

"Remember Uncle Jim and 'Amazing Grace'?" Julie said, pointing to where he'd stood that day.

"That slope isn't as steep as I thought; everything was bigger, then. I can still see him."

"You know, my mom told me that morning that he'd be playing his bagpipes sometime that day. She didn't say when. I remember being more surprised over how he changed clothes so fast. He must have changed out of his suit before leaving the funeral home."

*Jim Beecher in full Milwaukee
Highlander regalia
(Kortmann family photo,
photographer unknown)*

"Well, there *were* Clark Kent quick-change phone booths everywhere back then."

"Do you ever not have a quip?" she asked. "I know, I know, it's a Beecher thing." Her attention shifted to the view a few steps ahead. "Let's check out this row of graves."

There were four headstones, spaced equidistant: our great-great grandparents, Mary S. Clancy and Daniel P. Clancy, then great-grandparents Margaret Clancy-Beecher and August Beecher.

Julie stopped above Margaret's grave. "Did you know this is her wedding ring? My mom gave it to me in 1977 when I got married. It's really weird standing here with her ring on."

"I forgot all about that, but now that you mention it, I remember. How cool is that. Talk about coming full circle."

She took a knee, placing the fingers of her left hand on the top of our great-grandmother's stone, caressing the letters etching Margaret's name.

I resisted my urge to say, *that was touching*. It really was. When Julie stood, I put my arm around her. We smiled and hugged.

We walked around a 100-foot radius, noticing the adjacent gravestones bore names of mostly Irish nationality. Surveying the scenery from every angle triggered vague imagery from the funeral. Less vague, were the feelings rising inside me for my mother. Her visible grief that day, juxtaposed with the family truth I now knew had me in awe. Though her remains weren't located here, I felt her presence, her lightness, her forgiving nature and more than ever. Her strength.

"Oh yeah, I almost forgot," Julie said.

Her words snapped me back to the present. I turned and walked back to where she stood in the grassy space to the side of our grandfather's marker. She pulled out the burial plot diagram from her purse.

"Yikes," she said and then back peddled a few steps after becoming aware of where she had been standing. "This shows the wives are buried right here."

I donned my reading glasses for a closer look at the page in her hands. "Wow, no gravestones. Why would there be no gravestones?"

"I don't know, but that sucks," she said, shaking her head.

"No kidding. Unless maybe, could it have been a budget issue back then?" I wondered. "They both have stones. And they both have a stone," I said, pointing to the markers of our great-grandparents and the double-greats.

"I wish our mothers were alive and we could ask them."

"Maybe we should come back with a Ouija board."

Clancy-Beecher plot in Calvary Cemetery. Grandfather's grave at lower right.

A gust of wind forced us to steady our stances. "That wind is nuts. I can't believe how cold it got suddenly," I declared. "Let's take a few pictures get out of here."

"I can't believe this," Julie said, clearly dismayed. "This really creeps me out."

Before exiting the boneyard, we circled through the rest of the 65-acre cemetery. We talked about the family graves, especially the unmarked ones. Julie searched the web on her cell phone and located a cemetery tour guide that helped us locate graves of historic note, including that of Milwaukee's co-founder and first mayor Solomon Juneau, and Frederick Miller, the German immigrant who settled in Milwaukee and founded the Miller Brewing Company in 1855. Kind of fitting, the Old Boy had worked at Miller, drank Miller and now, here they were, Frederick and Carroll, their final resting places facing east, a one-mile crow's flight to the 164-year-old brewery.

An hour had passed since our arrival. I drove out of Calvary and pulled up behind Julie's car.

"Want to stop for a bite and a drink across the street before we split?"

"I think a proper cocktail is in order," she replied.

"Look at that, it's 49," I said, pointing to the temperature display on the dashboard. "It was 67 when we got here an hour ago. The sudden wind and the cold. It was like someone was telling us to mind our own business."

"Maybe it was someone telling us not to forget about them."

****

That was the weather that afternoon. You can look it up.

Our return to Calvary was profound. We knew there were disturbing things in our mothers' pasts. Long ago, we were told their mother had died from a broken heart. Then why, after her sad demise, would our grandfather put her *and* his second wife in the ground, sans the dignity of a grave marker? We already knew that his third wife, Demi, was buried elsewhere. Now, unwelcome thoughts of, let's say, unkind possibilities, seemed more real than ever. Our mothers must have known their mother's grave had no marker. Did they not care? Why wouldn't they?

5.

WAY BACK

"What famous date should I set it to today, Mr. Peabody?"
~Sherman the kid at the Wayback Machine asking Mr. Peabody,
the talking professor dog, on the Rocky & Bullwinkle Show. *Circa*
1959 or the year my grandfather gave me my first Kit Kat bar.

June 23, 1905. Carroll Augustine Beecher was born in Milwaukee, Wisconsin.

His mother, Margaret (birth name Margaretha), was second generation Irish. Her parents were Mary and Daniel Clancy. Daniel made his living as a saloon operator until he died in 1897.

Carroll's father, Augustino, worked as a telegraph operator. Augustino's father, August, was a German immigrant from the Kingdom of Prussia. August supported a politically liberal faction of Europeans known as Forty-Eighters. In the German Revolution, they failed in their bid to unify the Germanic states behind a more democratic government. Some Forty-Eighters, determined to find a better life, sailed across the Atlantic and settled in Wisconsin. August chose the Town of Herman in Dodge County, about 40 miles northwest of grandson Carroll's birthplace.

August's son, Augustino, died of pneumonia in 1909, leaving behind a young wife, four-year-old, Carroll, and a two-year-old daughter, Minette. Augustino was fond of calling his boy Butchie, derived from the German surname Bücher or Butcher. As a way of continuing her husband's presence, Margaret began calling her son Butchie and in time, simply Butch. She would call him Carroll only when she meant business.

With the household breadwinner gone, Margaret moved five miles south, from the area once known as North Milwaukee, to live with her mother, Mary Clancy, near 16th and Coldspring Avenue, known today as Highland Avenue.

Moving in with his Irish grandmother set the stage for Carroll's formative years. Fatherless Carroll had an uncle, James Clancy, who operated a saloon in a nearby Irish neighborhood known as Tory Hill, a rough neighborhood that reflected the hard-fought history of Irish Americans in Milwaukee.

Over a half-century earlier, Milwaukee's earliest European immigrants were the Irish, who'd fled the *Auld Sod* due to famine and oppressive English rule. Initially, they settled in the Third Ward, an area of reclaimed swampland between Lake Michigan and the Milwaukee River. As in all large American cities then, Milwaukee's Irish struggled for acceptance, languishing in low-paying, unskilled jobs and forced to live in squalor. Harsh conditions led to so much drunkenness and brawling, the area was dubbed the *Bloody Third.* As decades passed, Irish political leaders gradually earned respectability, paving the way for some to move westward, establishing the Tory Hill neighborhood. Its approximate borders were North 4th to North 13th Streets and from West Michigan Street down to the railroad tracks south of St. Paul Avenue. A hill that sloped to the Menomonee River Valley was the geographic focal point that inspired the area's name.

By the turn of the century, Tory Hill and adjacent neighborhoods were a densely populated, rugged mix of the city's two largest ethnic populations at the time, German and Irish.

It was unclear where young Butch began elementary school, but it was said he received an education in saloon life and *adventures* in the streets and alleyways. He had an instinct for finessing his way through encounters, even alternating his surname between Beecher and Clancy, whichever ethnicity created a situational advantage. His role models were Uncle James, along with older boys and men practiced in the manly pursuits of drinking alcohol and stealing whatever they wanted. By age 13, he was already a prolific drinker of any beer or booze he could get his hands on. People grew up fast in those days. At the turn of the century, the average life expectancy for an American male was 48.3. years. Being teen age was ambiguous then. For most males, you were a child; then you got a job, and you were an adult.

Margaret, who found work as a dressmaker, had noble hopes for her son's future. Part of the Irish American experience was the ongoing struggle to overcome the ruffian stereotype. Her dream was for Carroll to become a policeman, a growing Irish aspiration in America's major cities, from Boston to New York, Chicago and Milwaukee.

Around 1920, Margaret moved with her mother and two children to live in Merrill Park, another predominantly Irish neighborhood that had evolved along the Menomonee Valley corridor westward, beyond Tory Hill. Their new home was an apartment building on North 35th Street. It placed Margaret closer to her full-time dressmaking job on North 26th Street and farther from the environment she believed was pulling her son toward delinquency.

Had Margaret been clairvoyant, her worries might have been eased by the knowledge that in the years to follow, two boys close in age to Butch would emerge from local Irish street life to success and fame in show business – actors Pat O'Brien and Spencer Tracy.

Margaret continued to rely on a Catholic upbringing to keep her boy out of trouble. She enrolled Butch in St. Thomas Aquinas Catholic school at North 36th and Brown Streets. It was here where he most likely developed his chops in religious lampoonery. Later, Butch attended West Side High School, located at 22nd Street and Prairie, now known as Highland Avenue. Butch did not become a famous alum, in fact, I don't know whether he even finished high school.

My grandfather came of age at a time of dramatic social and political transformation in America. Three Constitutional changes to the law of the land were enacted in a seven-year stretch. The Sixteenth Amendment established a federal tax on income to fund the federal government. The 18th Amendment prohibited the manufacture, distribution and sale of alcohol, and the Nineteenth Amendment finally granted women's voting rights.

When his work life began in 1922, Margaret's hopes for her son's career were renewed by recent news of the city's new Police Training Academy. Known as the first municipal police training school in the world, it was established by Police Chief, Jacob Laubenheimer, who became chief of the 12th largest city in the U.S. at the tender age of 28, in 1921.

Butch eschewed his mum's latest exhortation to make his living as a policeman, telling her, "Ma, I won't be a good cop if I have to arrest people for drinking."

Instead, he continued to earn paychecks working as an attendant at a Standard Oil Company gas station. One interesting tidbit I found in old records showed he also worked for a short time as a clerk at Benjamin Schwartz, a floral shop somewhere in Milwaukee.

Sometime during this period Butch reconnected with a rascal

from his Tory Hill days, known only as Tommy Boy. Tommy was a few years older and, like Butch, was German/Irish with a rebellious streak. A teenage petty thief turned Prohibition opportunist, Tommy made a living in bootlegging, the underground industry that quickly flourished when the Eighteenth Amendment establishing Prohibition had taken effect three years earlier.

No city in the United States had a drinking culture more deep-seated than Milwaukee, home to nine breweries and over 2,000 saloons when the 1920s began. In the previous decade during World War I, Milwaukee's culture faced anti-German sentiment. America's Anti-Saloon League called Milwaukee and its many breweries "the worst of all our German enemies," labeling Milwaukee beer as "Kaiser Brew." For decades, the American Temperance Movement viewed Milwaukee as a shameful den of iniquity. Carrie Nation, the movement's longtime icon, famed for attacking alcohol-serving establishments with a hatchet, once said, "If there is any place that is hell on earth, it is Milwaukee."

Butch was the same age his grandfather had been while fighting against government oppression in Europe. With rebellion in his blood, the allure of earning unreported, untaxed income while defying an unjust Prohibition law proved irresistible. The seductive trappings of Tommy Boy's world secretly now occupied much of Butch's time on nights and weekends.

6.

FOLKLORE

*"The only thing more fun than drinking in those days was
helping people drink against the law." - Tommy Boy*

B y the end of 1924, Butch cut his work hours at the Standard
station in favor of driving Tommy's Ford Model-T truck.

Tommy was a supplier of the "speakeasy," hidden saloons
disguised as cafes, soda shops and a variety of entertainment venues.
The term for the speakeasy arose from the practice to speak quietly,
or speak easy, about such a place in public or when inside it, so as
not to alert the police and neighbors. His portfolio of speakeasy
customers throughout Milwaukee was now more than he could
handle alone. He had his system of delivery and collection down
cold. He and *Big Daddy*, Tommy's nickname for Butch, divvied
the workload. Most of the time, Tommy ran deliveries within the
city on weekdays to longtime speakeasy operators, several of which
were frequented by some of Milwaukee's social and political elite.
Butch took his turns making pickups and deliveries on nights and
weekends.

How much of their exploits were fact or fiction can never be proven. Regarding his new partner, Tommy looked back on those days' decades later.

"He really took to it. Fit the part, got all spiffed, striped three-piece suit, collar bar, looked like a real big shot. The kid was low key, but I'll tell you, he had charisma," Tommy mused. "First time out, I look him up and down. He's sharp as a tack. All he says is, *BEATS PUMPIN' GAS*. He had this deadpan humor. Quick. Really cracked me up."

Carroll "Butch" Beecher – c. 1920s

One particular story retold decades later stood out. Allegedly, it involved a two-night marathon Tommy called the *Legend of Count Butch Orlok*, a reference to the vampire named Orlok in the 1922 German silent horror film, *Nosferatu*. Butch did not suck blood, nor did he retreat to a coffin in daylight. What he could do was get by on little sleep when opportunities for debauchery were ripe for the eating.

First stop: a warehouse and speakeasy in Hartford, thirty-five miles northwest of Milwaukee. Once there, he headed for the speak, an extra room built beyond the warehouse office, where he was sure to encounter a few Friday night regulars. Among them were two rural flapper wannabees, Lily and Rose. Arrival of the handsome, well-dressed young man from Milwaukee became their weekly highlight.

"There he is!" exclaimed Lily.

"Well, hello, Big Daddy," chimed Rose.

He walked over to greet her with a hug and a kiss for Lily, then one for Rose, sitting on the adjoining bar stool. Tending bar was a man Butch had not met before, though he had heard things about the suave young man from Milwaukee who'd come to the warehouse for a big Friday load. He reached out to shake Butch's hand.

"Hello, Butch, I'm Jack. Nice to meet you. I know your Uncle Charlie up in Mayville."

"Small world," Butch replied. "So, you know Charlie, eh? When I was a kid, I stayed at his farm in the summer a few times. From what I hear, the old hound is still quite the cake-eater (lady's man)."

"From what I hear, it runs in the family. Let me fix you a Gin Rickey before you load up."

"Sounds jake, Jack. I got time for one or more."

"Count us in for another," Lily added, her words slurred from prior Rickey's.

Jack mixed three and served them. He mixed one for himself and turned to offer a toast. "Here's to you, Butch, Big Daddy, whoever the hell you are."

Before long, they adjourned through a door with a makeshift sign – PETTING ZOO. My, oh, my. When the zoo door reopened, three creatures meandered out after a gratifying romp in the wild.

"I wish I didn't have to leave. What do I owe you, chief?" Butch asked Jack.

"Not a damn thing, Butch. Just glad you're on our team."

With a wink and a nod, Big Daddy headed out to make his appointed rounds southeast.

He delivered to clubs, speaks and homes of the well-to-do in Oconomowoc, Pewaukee and then on to Brookfield, to a place he talked of in his later years. It was called Club Madrid, a free-wheeling night club, about 10 miles west of Milwaukee, located at 12600 West Bluemound Road. Dapper owner, Sam Pick, offered fine food, black market booze, dancing and music. Vices involving gambling and women were known to be available upstairs. Brookfield had no police department then. County sheriffs looked the other way. It was Roaring 20's heaven where Butch spent time that night with a woman he was quite familiar with. Her name was Betty.

After some bobbing and weaving in Brookfield, Butch continued east into Milwaukee County. There were more stops in West Allis and West Milwaukee, where third shift workers would soon be punching out, in search of a drink at one of the many neighborhood speakeasies masked as soda shops and grocery stores. His last delivery was at the foot of the towering silos of the Kurth Malting Plant on South 43rd Street. He drove his truck to the far end of the building to the transport docks, where his man Max stood smoking a Chesterfield. Max played baseball with Butch. He made a nice side income selling Butch's whiskey to scores of men working at Kurth, as well as the huge Hotpoint appliance manufacturing plant across the street.

"Nice to see your face for a change instead of Tommy's ugly mug," Max joked.

"Without your baseball cap, you're uglier than usual, pal," jibed Butch. "Butt me, will ya? I'm out of Lucky's."

Max pulled a Chesterfields pack from his jacket and shook one loose.

Butch lit up, tilted his head back to exhale and grinned. "Now, give me a C and a half and you can have whatever I have left in back."

"A hundred and fifty clams? What, am I a sucker all of a sudden?"

"You should eyeball all the hooch I've got for you before you start belly aching."

Max climbed in the back of the truck, sifting through the straw that cushioned bottles in the open crates. He hopped out. "We're copasetic after all. You're lucky I got enough dough."

"You're lucky you got pals like me and Tommy," Butch cracked. "I'll help you unload. Then, I got a banana to deliver."

"Banana?"

"Yeah. You know the blond skirt in the stands at Washington Park?"

"Sure. that's Anna. The one with the big bubs."

"She's waiting to serve me breakfast. I'll serve her my banana."

Max shook his head and chuckled in amazement. "I don't know how you do it. You're a sheik."

Butch winked. "Talk softly and carry a big stick, my friend. See you at Washington on Sunday, Maxie."

"See ya, Butch. Thanks for the hooch. Say hello to Tommy for me."

After breakfast and a *nap* with Anna, he left around noon and drove to a warehouse next to the Milwaukee Electric Railway and Light Company's power plant on Commerce Street, along the banks of the Milwaukee River. There, he met Angelo, a heavyweight in local bootlegging and a meticulously organized distributor of gin, whiskey and other liquors. Months earlier, Butch recoiled at working with Tommy's Italian supplier.

"I'm not going to be a fart catcher for a goddamned dago."

Tommy reminded his junior partner of the big picture. "Hey, Prohibition is bullshit, right? We believe in the right to drink, right? So does Angelo. Who cares if he's a Guinea? It's us against the feds. He's on our side. C'mon, I vouched for you with the guy. This is what you signed up for. I can't do it all alone."

Not only did Butch relent after Tommy's pep talk, he came to appreciate the modus operandi of Angelo's Commerce Street enterprise. Wooden cases were coded, filled, and staged just inside a dock bay door when Butch or Tommy arrived. A nameless, coded manifest listed addresses and collection instructions corresponding to all the coded cases. Every driver got the speech from Angelo their first time out:

"Make your deliveries within the time frame assigned.
No lollygagging. No drinking on my dime.
No stops for brothel bops. Your pay gets docked for breakage.
Miss a delivery, you're fired. If you catch any heat,
keep your mouth shut. You don't know me."

Angelo, who believed a neat appearance helped avoid scrutiny, required his men to dress in a suit and fedora. "Look professional, act professional. I charge top dollar to my customers. I want them to feel they're getting their money's worth, right down to the men who bring the goods."

A driver had better have a good reason for a misstep. Cross Angelo and you'd soon find yourself confronted by a tandem of Bruno's proficient at securing restitution and meting out punitive damage.

By mid-afternoon, Butch began hitting delivery points concentrated in a 10-mile radius – Brady Street, Lake Drive, the downtown red-light district along Wells Street from the

Milwaukee River to 6th Street, then west to mansions on Highland and Wisconsin Avenues.

Seven hours later, Butch returned to the warehouse, his briefcase filled with envelopes containing cash and checks. Two of Angelo's men were there; one counted the take from the briefcase while the other poured Butch a shot of whiskey.

"We're good, kid. Here's your end," said the count man, who handed Butch his envelope of cash.

———

Anna had promised to have a surprise waiting for him. When he arrived a few minutes before midnight, Butch entered her unlocked door. She approached in come-hither frillies, her right arm bent upward in a 90-degree angle and a lit cigarette elegantly propped in her fingers.

"Here you go. I know you prefer Lucky's," she purred, placing the cigarette in his mouth.

"I like your idea of surprises," replied Butch, his eyes fixed on all of her, as she removed his suit coat and tie.

"Only half of the surprise, my tall, dark and handsome friend," Anne took him by the hand and led him to the bedroom door. When she pushed the door open, his eyes widened at the sight of a long-haired brunette woman, lying provocatively on Anna's bed. "You remember Dottie, don't you?"

"How could I forget?" Butch answered with a sly smile.

"I'll be right back with a cold beer for you."

"Thanks, Anna. I'm starving. You got anything to eat?"

"I've got some pie and leftover chicken in the ice box. Climb in with Dottie. I'll be right back."

Moments later, they were a trio *in the bare scud.* He was fed like a king while he quaffed from a ceramic Mader's beer stein. Perhaps there was more bobbing and weaving and sharing of cherry pie in ways that gave new meaning to the word "dessert."

As Butch readied to leave later that morning, Anna extended an open invitation. "Come see us anytime, Butch. Always a cold growler or two waiting in the box."

Maybe Max was right. Maybe Butch really was a sheik.

Soon, a favor for his mother would lead the Sheik to a Sheba worth courting.

7.

SMITTEN

Margaret was sick. Butch ventured out with his mother's short-list of sundries. To ease her bronchial torment, one item topped her list – Veno's Lightning Cough Cure was at the top of her list.

"The one place you're sure to find it is Weigle & Schevves," she said, referring to her favorite drugstore in their former neighborhood.

Butch threw on a hat and overcoat, braving frigid temperatures as he waited to climb aboard an eastbound Grand Avenue streetcar.

Noon bells tolled from the church across the street as he opened the drug store's glass door. Here, on a sunny, ice cold Saturday in January 1925, fate intersected with destiny at the corner of 12th and Grand.

Once inside, his eyes were drawn to the hotsy-totsy brunette to his right, waiting on a patron at the register. He stopped in his tracks, mesmerized by her milky white complexion, perfectly blushed cheeks and seductive red lips. As she began bagging her customer's purchases, her hazel brown eyes met the piercing baby blues of the tall, handsome man gazing her way. She looked back at her customer momentarily, then back at Butch as he began to step away. He turned his head to peek at her one more time. Her eyes were still on him.

At that moment, he knew, and she knew. Their animal chemistry was unmistakable.

Butch made haste, quickly scanning shelves and plucking the items on his list. He walked back toward the cashier. She had no customer to wait on and appeared to be preoccupied with straightening her already neat work area in an awkward attempt to avoid looking his way. When Butch stood before her, she slowly raised her head to see his captivating blue eyes and gentle smile up close. With her heart pounding, she gave her usual greeting.

"Hello, how are you today?" she asked, mirroring his smile.

"Fine," replied Butch, nodding as his smile grew.

"I'm picking up some things for my mother."

"Oh my, I'm sorry; I hope she's not feeling too badly," Marie said with a look of concern as she glanced over his purchases.

"I'm sure it's just a bad cold. She'll be fine. If you don't mind my asking, do you live around here?"

"Yes, I do," Marie said, adding, "I go to Gesu, right across the street." Translation: *I'm a proper young Catholic woman, and I don't share my particulars at the drop of a hat, Mister Blue Eyes.* She was referring to Church of the Gesu at 1145 Grand Avenue, known by locals as simply, Gesu.

"Oh, really? I go there, too," said Butch, mentally crossing his fingers, knowing it had been years since he'd last attended Mass at Gesu with his mother. "What Sunday Mass do you usually go to?"

"The 10 o'clock: High Mass."

"Ah, well, I go to the last Mass at 12:15. That explains why I haven't seen you there. If I did, I wouldn't forget such a beautiful face." Butch was lucky to even remember Gesu's schedule, never mind the fact that he had never been to a 12:15 service in his life.

Their chat was forced to a quick conclusion when an older woman stepped up behind Butch.

"My name is Butch. Well, actually it's Carroll, but I go by Butch."

"I'm Marie. It was nice to meet you. Thanks. Have a wonderful day."

"Thank YOU. I'm sure I'll see you again."

Marie smiled, blushed, and nodded.

Sheba – A woman with sex appeal (slang popularized by the 1921 movie, *Queen of Sheba*).

Spellbound Butch had just met Marie Cecelia Leicht (pronounced "Light").

Marie Leicht c. 1922
(Photo via Martin Weirich genealogical archive)

Marie was born in Milwaukee on April 10, 1904, the first child of Cecelia Greenwald and John Baptist Leicht, who'd married the previous June. Both parents were of German ancestry. Their home stood at the corner of N. 21st Street and Grand Avenue. In 1907, the couple had a second daughter, Dorothy.

When Marie was seven, her mother died during childbirth at age 34. The baby survived and was named Agnes. John Leicht persevered through tragedy, eventually marrying Patricia Norris in 1917. They had a son, John, the following year. Patricia was said to have been a fine wife and loving stepmother.

John was a thoughtful, intelligent man and a devout Catholic. He was a school master, teaching general studies and music. He was also a gifted musician, the principal organist and music director at Gesu, the very church Marie pointed out to Butch in their first conversation.

Nine months earlier, after Marie's twentieth birthday, it was John who granted Marie permission to take her first job outside the house, at the drug store in the shadow of Gesu, his home away from home.

———————————

The morning after meeting Marie, Butch donned his best suit. Impeccably attired, he hoped to slip out undetected. Nope. Margaret, who was in the kitchen hunched over a pot of boiled water to steam open her sinuses, peeked out from her chair just in time to catch a glimpse toward the front door.

"Whoa, whoaaa! Hold yer horses there, Butchie Boy. Where the heck are ya goin' on a Sunday mornin' dressed like that?"

Butch froze, the expression of a boy caught with his hand in the cookie jar all over his mug. Despite pausing, he could come up with no bullshit off the top of his head. When a young man's dick is doing all the thinking, that'll happen.

"I'm going to church."

"Really now, are ya?" Margaret replied with incredulous

curiosity. "Well, it's a miracle. I been praying all mornin' fer God to fergive me for not goin' to church. Why, he musta give me a miracle!"

By now, Butch had closed the door to stop the cold from pouring in, still speechless with a sheepish half-grin.

"There's only one explanation. It must be a girl," Margaret said with certainty. Her son looked back at her with a forced smile. "Gotta go, Ma. Can I get you anything?"

"You just did."

Mother Margaret watched her son go out the door. The unexpected gift of her son voluntarily dressed for church on a Sunday morning helped her lose track of her chest congestion.

A streetcar ride later, Butch entered Gesu Church and took a spot in a back pew for the 10 a.m. High Mass. When services ended, he stood purposefully adjacent to the huge doorways as worshipers exited. Eventually, Marie and her sisters came forth. Butch smiled as their eyes met.

"Well, good morning, Carroll. Did you enjoy your first 10 a.m. Mass?" Marie asked with a wry grin.

"Best Mass I've been to in years," he said cheerfully.

"I see," was Marie's *you're full of baloney* reply. "Oh. Let me introduce you to my sisters. This is Dorothy, and this is Agnes."

Butch smiled and gave each sister a single nod, hat still in hand. "My pleasure."

The two teenage girls smiled and nodded back, then looked impishly at their star-struck sister.

"Will I see you again next Saturday at the drug store?"

"You will, but it's actually my last day there."

"Really? How so?"

"If I see you on Saturday, I might tell you then. It was nice to see you again, Carroll."

"Likewise," Butch answered, tantalized by her invitation and impressed she remembered his formal name. "Would you mind telling me when you finish work?"

"Five o'clock."

Feeling it too presumptuous to walk out with Marie, Butch opted to stay right where he was until Marie disappeared. As she moved further away, her sisters looked back at Butch, then looked at each other and giggled.

That next Saturday, January 31, dapper Butch entered the drug store a few minutes before 5 p.m., clad in a tan three-piece suit, topped with a black overcoat and a tan-banded black fedora.

"Hello, Marie. Were you worried I wouldn't show up?"

"Well, hello, Carroll and no, I wasn't worried. After all, you did ask when I'd be finished working, right?"

He smiled with a self-amused nod. "I guess I tipped my hand."

"I like the hand you're playing, so far. Would you mind waiting for a few minutes.? I have to close things up."

"Sure, I'll wait outside."

Butch puffed a Lucky outside, while Marie went about her final duties. Halfway through his second Lucky, Marie came out the door with the store's co-owner, pharmacist George Weigle.

"Now, don't be a stranger, Marie," George said, extending his hand for a farewell handshake.

"You know I won't, sir," Marie replied as she shook his hand.

George looked at Butch. "I'm closing up, sir. Can I help you?"

"I'm waiting for Marie."

George's eyes shifted from Butch to Marie, who flashed *a look what I found* smile.

"Ah, I see," declared George. "Well, I'll say this, young man. I've seen a lot of drug store cowboys out here over the years. You're the cream of the crop." George extended his hand. "Vestis facit virum."

With a half-hearted smile, Butch shook George's hand, bamboozled by whatever the pharmacist had just said to him.

George receded, shutting the door and flipping his door sign to CLOSED.

Anxious to know, Butch asked "What the heck did he just say?"

"It's Latin for Clothes make the man."

"Huh. Why didn't he just say so? I speak a little Latin, too, you know. Ah-na-way, oh-gay, out-yay, for inner-day?"

Marie laughed heartily at his pig-Latin witticism. "That would be nice, but I can't go out with you dressed in work clothes. Look at you, you're dressed to kill."

"Is it working?"

Evidently so. Marie agreed to a cup of coffee. They walked to a Grand Avenue diner one block away.

"I can't stay long. If I'm not home by 6 o'clock, my father will be worried."

"So, where do you live? Tell me about your family."

"There's six of us. We live on 21st Street. It's my father, my two sisters you saw at church, my stepmother and stepbrother."

"What about your mother?"

"She died in 1911."

"Sorry. That's tough. I know. My father died in 1909."

"I'm sorry to hear that, Carroll." Marie paused, looking him straight in the eyes. "It's quite a thing to have in common, isn't it?"

He nodded with a hint of melancholy. "Life goes on."

"How about you? Do you still live at home, too?"

"Yeah, with my mother and sister. Grandmother, too. We're up on 35th Street."

"And what do you do?"

"I work at a gas station. I do some delivery driving on the side."

"Hmmm. Sounds like you're a busy man."

"So, are you going to keep working?"

"Oh my, yes. I can't wait. I start Monday as a teller at First

National Bank downtown on Water Street. Perhaps you can come see me there, too."

"I'd love to do that, if that's what it takes to get you to go out with me. Can I bank on it?"

Marie tittered, rolling her eyes and perhaps, increasingly impressed with his quick wit. "You are something else, Carroll."

"Really, you can call me Butch. Never cared for the name Carroll. When I hear it, someone's mad at me . . . or trying to get my goat."

"Well, I hope it never comes to that, Butch. Can I bank on that?"

He nodded, perhaps equally impressed by her quick-comeback abilities.

"If I open my heart to you, promise me. Say you won't break my heart. Ever."

"Sure," he said, caught off guard by her weighty request. "I will never break your heart."

****

Their first date was Saturday, February 14. Seven months later, they gathered with family and friends across from the drug store where they met. The Gesu church bells would toll for them.

8.

MATRIFIED

Labor Day. Monday, September 7, 1925, Carroll August Beecher and Marie Cecelia Leicht married at Church of the Gesu.

Marie wanted a summer wedding. Butch did not want his summer schedule disturbed. Much of his Saturday hours were dedicated to bootlegging affairs with Tommy Boy. On Sundays, he was a force to be reckoned with while armed with a bat and mitt in some of the city's most competitive baseball circuits. The couple proposed Labor Day as a unique alternative to both Father Terrence Devlin, Gesu's pastor, and Marie's father, John. The men gave their blessing, and Marie fancied the notion of future wedding anniversaries doubling as a national holiday.

Gesu was among the city's architectural jewels and a prized wedding venue for any young Catholic couple. Its impressive French Gothic-style was inspired by the cathedrals of France and its two-tower façade struck a dramatic silhouette that could be seen for miles. This was the wedding Marie had dreamed of – a holy, Catholic ceremony in the same church where her parents had been united in the sacrament of marriage in 1903.

At twenty-one, Marie was luminous in the streamlined, white silhouette gown style coveted by modern-minded brides of the era. Her brunette bobbed hair was covered by a Juliet cap veil.

Butch looked like a silent film leading man in his black suit, white vest and a steel blue necktie and pocket scarf that matched the black-banded fedora he arrived in. John would be giving away his daughter in one-of-a-kind fashion – as both father of the bride and ceremony organist. He had served as Gesu's organist-in-residence since 1896 and had gained local notoriety for his mastery of Gesu's mighty Kimball pipe organ. Originally built by W.W. Kimball Company in the 1890's, the organ was acquired by church officials from the Studebaker Theater in Chicago and installed in the church in 1908. The organ had approximately 50 ranks, in four divisions, totaling nearly 3,000 pipes.

John played three prelude songs, the last being Pachelbel's Canon in D. Then, his understudy sat in, and he dashed down the stairs to walk his daughter down the aisle. Marie and her father processed to the resounding glory of "Here Comes the Bride." Marie and many onlookers fought back tears of joy as she floated toward Butch, waiting at the foot of Gesu's grand altar. Their ceremony unfolded without a hitch. Well, except for the hitching part.

> Father Devlin: Carroll, do you take Marie for your lawful wife, to have and to hold, from this day forward, for better, for worse, for richer, for poorer, in sickness and in health, until death do you part?
> Butch: I do.
> Father Devlin: Marie, do you take Carroll for your lawful husband, to have and to hold, from this day forward, for better, for worse, for richer, for poorer, in sickness and in health, until death do you part?
> Marie: I do.
> Father Devlin: What God joins together, let no man put asunder.

There was the blessing of rings and some closing hocus pocus, all witnessed by a sizable throng of family, friends and parishioners, a testament to the joy so many wanted to share with John Leicht's esteemed family. Gesu's mighty Kimball pipes bellowed the triumphant sound of Mendelssohn's "Wedding March" as Milwaukee's freshest married couple strolled arm-in-arm toward the dramatic triple-arched portico doorways leading to Grand Avenue.

Once they passed the huge open doors, they found the morning sun had given way to gloomy skies and storm clouds approaching from the west. Fearing rain, the newlyweds decided to greet their guests in the vestibule instead of outside. After nearly an hour of meeting with well-wishers, the happy couple stepped out the main doors, pleased to find that not a drop had fallen. Of rain, that is. A drop *did* fall and splatted on Marie's gown. A "gift" from above, courtesy of a crow perched atop the cement archway that towered above the double doors. As Marie tried to laugh it off, Dorothy, Marie's sister and maid of honor, rushed off and returned with a wet rag to save the day.

From there, the wedding party climbed into a brand new 1925 Nash 4-door sedan, lent to Butch by an acquaintance of Tommy Boy, a well-to-do operator of several Milwaukee speakeasies. Made by Nash Motors in nearby Kenosha, it was a roomy, burgundy five-passenger with a tan canvas top. It was a stylish step up from the used, *Tin Lizzy* Model T Ford that Butch had recently bought.

They began their celebratory ride, rolling east on Grand Avenue, Milwaukee's main street. Butch squeezed the car's manual horn repeatedly, weaving through a maze of other vehicles, streetcars and horse-drawn vendor carts that filled the street, even on a holiday. Marie, Dorothy and best man Tommy, smiled and waved to amused onlookers.

"Woo-hoo!" howled Tommy, booze flask in one hand, waving with the other.

"Butch, slow down a bit," said Marie. "Isn't the new Gimbels something?" she declared, pointing to the completely rebuilt Gimbels Department Store on their right, originally opened at Grand and Plankinton Avenues by Bavarian Jewish immigrant, Adam Gimbel. "I ride the streetcar past here every day to and from the bank. The streets around here are always crawling with people."

They rolled under the Court of Neptune archway above the Milwaukee River bridge.

"That's where I work," Marie said, pointing right again, this time toward the First National Bank. "I love just looking out the window at work at those amazing columns on the new Gimbels building across the river. I love working there."

"How about you pilfer some lettuce for me one of these days," Tommy joked.

Their drive of nearly two miles culminated at the Lake Michigan overlook plaza on the south end of picturesque Outer Memorial Drive.

Dorothy had her father's Leica I camera, the latest state-of-the-art camera made in Germany. Sunlight peaked through, just in time for the couples to photograph each other with Lake Michigan glistening in the background. As they celebrated, bodacious Butch produced his trusty flask and the four shared sips of *panther piss*, otherwise known as Wisconsin bootleg whiskey.

"Did you have that in your pocket during our ceremony?" Marie asked incredulously.

Butch said nothing, responding with a wink and his patented double raised eyebrow wiggle.

The four piled into the Nash and resumed their horn-honking celebration on wheels. Just before 5:00 p.m., they arrived at their reception destination on North 4th Street. Turner Hall was another of Milwaukee's architectural gems. Built in 1882 by German immigrants' intent on reproducing the Romanesque Revival design they missed from their homeland, Turner's was among the city's swankier joints.

John Leicht dropped a chunk of his savings to ensure his daughter's wedding was the bee's knees, with one exception. He refused to pay for any alcohol. It's not that he never took a drink himself, he simply would not put his reputation at risk. With some advance coaxing by Marie and Butch, John agreed to allow alcohol in, providing the groom's family covered the cost. A dry reception was out of the question for Butch. He assured John that his uncle, Charles, agreed to cover the cost. In truth, Charles contributed nothing toward the cost of beer and the hard stuff. Old Uncle Charlie was part of a ploy concocted by Butch to make his new father-in-law believe the Beecher family had furnished the alcohol. Charlie would not have driven all the way down from Mayville without assurance of free beer awaiting him in Milwaukee. Weeks earlier, Butch talked things through with Charlie.

"Look, John's a fine man and all, but he's a bit of a blue nose. I just want you to help me make it look like we're doing the right thing, ya' follow?"

"Fine. Whatever. Christ sakes, it ain't a wedding party without beer."

Even at the tender age of 20, Butch was already proficient at the art of the ruse. It was Butch himself who bore the cost of alcohol for his party. He "paid" by bartering his time and his truck in service to his bootlegging buddies.

Gaining cooperation of the hall operator and bartenders was easy. They could drink free, too, courtesy of the groom. If police made an unexpected visit, Turner's manager was accustomed to getting the coppers to turn a blind eye. Some cops were assuaged with a free drink; others had to be bought off with a bottle of take-home hooch.

Two roasted pigs were brought in for the evening's repast.

German potato salad, bakery and other homemade foods were brought in by dozens of women attending as guests.

Dorothy and Tommy each proposed a toast to the bride and groom.

Next, Marie spoke. "I want to thank you all from the bottom of my heart. Your being here means so much to me, and I know in my heart that my mother is looking down on us from heaven and is celebrating with us today. Thank you all, so very much."

Her words prompted heartfelt applause as Marie sat down. The applause continued, with some guests rising to their feet, prompting Marie to rise again in acknowledgement. She needed to pause, covering her face with a hand to quell her emotions.

"Thank you all again. It's Carroll's turn to do a toast. My advice to you now is to make sure your glasses are full. You're going to need it."

In one minute, Marie took everyone from tears to laughter.

Finally, Butch rose to toast their guests, including the Clancy's, his maternal Irish relatives in attendance. Chief among them was Butch's grandmother, Mary, the Clancy matriarch, and his own mother, Margaret, who'd branded her boy in 1905 with the Gaelic name Carroll, the Anglicized byname for a butcher or fierce warrior. He offered three toasts, each toast requiring its own tip of the glass.

"First, to everyone! Thank you all for coming."

His second toast was in German. "Keine Sorge, glücklich sein, eins, zwei, drei, trinken, Prost!" (Don't worry, be happy, one, two, three, drink, cheers!)

His third toast was to the Irish. "To the Clancys! Sláinte! (the Gaelic toast, for good health). May you live to be a hundred years, with one extra year to repent. Cheers!"

Butch had three full beer steins lined up in front of him on his place at the head table. His drinking prowess was on full display, as he dispatched a full stein of beer after each of his toasts. The raucous cheers of his guests grew with each chug.

Afterward, some of the ballroom tables were cleared to make way for a four-man band.

Merriment began with the traditional bride and groom's first dance, to the tune of, "It Had to Be You." Just before their dance ended, Marie's father, John, cut in to dance, and the band deftly switched to the Ted Weems hit, "Somebody Stole My Gal."

Butch and his mother, Margaret, were poised to immediately follow-up with their dance, "When Irish Eyes Are Smiling." The versatile quartet played a short set of traditional waltzes. Most of the older folk seized their chance to dance the old-fashioned way. They knew what was coming – the raucous rag time jazz that was all the rage during the Roaring Twenties.

It was time for the younger set to commandeer the center of the ballroom. They danced to the hits of the era: "Everybody Loves My Baby," "King Porter Stomp," the banjo boogie of "Bugle Call Rag." They did the Margie Fox Trot and multiple renditions of the dance that was all the rage, "The Charleston."

Marie proved to be quite the hoofer. Her puritan father looked on with smiling amazement. John had no idea that his daughter could dance like a flapper.

Meanwhile, bootleg beer continued to flow. When it came to gala events in Milwaukee, the Volstead Act was no match for Milwaukee's cultural traditions.

As the number of guests dwindled, Butch beseeched the remaining men, insisting they drink until the last beer barrel emptied. When the band finished for the night, they joined the diehard bulls at the trough. Surprisingly, Tommy abstained. To honor Marie's request for a dignified exit, he sat patiently near the exit doors after the music stopped, waiting to drive the newlyweds away. Once the last suds gurgled out, Marie convinced Butch it was finally time to go. Tommy drove the couple to the Milwaukee Hotel, just four blocks away on North 3rd Street. Once inside the penthouse suite atop the 19-floor inn, Butch plopped face first onto the largest bed they had ever seen.

"I'm matrified."

"What did you say, sweetheart?"

"We're matrified now. Big mattress."

Marie laughed. "Whatever you say, dear."

Butch began to snore. Marie succumbed in a way she hadn't anticipated. Instead of consummation, she settled for pulling off his shoes and getting herself ready for bed.

As her adrenaline subsided, Marie melted into a Victorian chair aside east facing windows. Gazing over a maze of rooftop silhouettes and the black void of Lake Michigan beyond, fresh glories of her grandest day settled into her memory and heart with one exception – the eyes of the crow that marred her first steps conjoined with Carroll August Beecher.

9.

CAROL AND FRET

1926. Their first home was a lower flat near North 34ᵗʰ Street and Lisbon Avenue. As the month of June approached, Marie was on the verge of motherhood. After a doctor confirmed she was pregnant in January, she'd bid farewell to her job at First National Bank and her short-lived life as a working woman earning a paycheck.

As Butch put it, "Once you're pregnant, no wife of mine is going to be out working a job with my bun in her oven."

Everyone focused on Marie. Grandparents-to-be, Margaret, John and Marie's stepmother Patricia were ecstatic. Despite the contrast in personalities between the biological grandparents, gregarious Margaret and soft-spoken John were said to have enjoyed each other's company. They shared a mutual respect from having raised children after untimely spousal deaths.

Marie spent the last few months engrossed in talks with her the younger sisters, "aunts-in-waiting," who seemed to have no end of questions:

How are you feeling? Did you feel it moving? Are you taking more naps? How much weight have you gained? Are you still getting sick? You should drink more milk. I can't believe how beautiful your skin is! Get some fresh air. Have you thought about names? Maybe you should bottle feed? You should breastfeed; it's natural. Get exercise. Stay off your feet. Who are you going to have midwife? The Gesu nuns can do it. Women are having babies at hospitals now, less painful. Don't worry.

On Wednesday, June 2, my mother, Carol Marie Beecher became the first person in the Beecher-Leicht lineage born in a hospital, rather than at home. In the unofficial competition of fertility and legitimate baby-making, Marie birthed her first child, nine months and five days after marriage, surpassing her mother's pace of nine months and 17 days after marrying John.

With the near constant presence of the family's six baby-loving females just a short streetcar ride away, Marie had all the support she could hope for. Butch was rarely home. He still worked his gas station job but limited his hours to keep his official annual income under the $3,000 threshold required for reporting to the Internal Revenue Service. He was now spending more time in Tommy's world. Making extra dough. Still, oats to sew.

Six months later, Marie and Butch opted for a night on the town to ring in 1927. For a late Friday night out, Dorothy was not Marie's go-to sitter; she was her go-to nanny. The word *babysitter* did not make its way into the American lexicon until the 1930s. The term first appeared in the Oxford English Dictionary in 1937.

Their destination – the Merrill Theater, was in bustling downtown Milwaukee, located at 211 West Wisconsin Avenue. Coincidentally, 11 days earlier, city fathers renamed the city's premiere thoroughfare from Grand Avenue to Wisconsin Avenue, a change that had been hotly debated for years and opposed by many Grand Avenue merchants.

Marie and Butch saw *The Temptress*, a silent movie hit, starring Greta Garbo. The Swedish born bombshell had quickly become a top box office attraction. Greta brought out the wolf in Butch. Marie noticed.

"You've got the hots for her, don't you?" Marie jibed Butch as they exited the Merrill.

He said nothing, responding only with his usual double raised eyebrow wiggle, garnished with a Cheshire cat grin. Marie countered with an eye roll of her own as they stepped side-by-side in haste to escape the cold and jump into their car.

It was their first time out on the town since Carol was born. Butch wanted to make the most of it. Earlier that week, he'd heard through Tommy of some private New Year's parties where alcohol would be plentiful. He drove a short eight-blocks east to the Lincoln Hotel. Built in the 1880s, the exterior of the six-story Lincoln had lost its luster. Once inside, they passed the front desk and the benign soda fountain that had once served as a saloon. Butch followed Tommy's instructions.

"Go down the first-floor hallway to Room 105. Knock five times. A guy will let you in and take you to the *Blind Pig*."

Suddenly, the Beechers were amid a New Year's Eve party in full quiver – juice, jazz and women adorned in the latest flapper apparel. Marie was amazed by the spectacle of it all and, in the moments that followed, by her man's familiarity with the ladies.

"Hi, Butchie! Good to see you," greeted a lively young woman, followed by an equally inebriated lass in a shimmering dress. "Is this your wife?" asked lively lady.

"Yes, it is. Ladies, this is Marie," said Butch, who turned to his wife. "Marie, this is Anna, and this is Dottie, same name as your sister."

Ill at ease, Marie said hello with a forced smile and reddened face. Butch shouldered his way to the bar, escorting Marie by the hand. She couldn't help looking back at the cackling coquettes. While Butch ordered cocktails, she scanned the spectacle of revelers in glad rags churning under glistening chandeliers to the sound of a jazz quintet. Five white musicians in formal attire were tightly clustered on a makeshift stage, scatting out their version of Louie Armstrong's, "Heebie Jeebies."

Butch regained his bride's attention, handing her a cocktail glass. "Try this. It's called the *Bee's Knees*. The barkeep calls it the drink of the night for the ladies. Gin, honey and lemon."

Marie tasted it. "Not bad, actually. What do you have there?"

"I ordered a *Gin Rickey*, heavy. It's lemon, club soda and heavy on the gin."

"I've had beer before, but this is my first cocktail ever."

"It's about time. Here's to you, Ree! Prost!"

Marie recoiled slightly after her inaugural sip. "This is really something. I've been to a few wedding receptions but nothing like this."

"Just helping you make up for lost time," Butch replied. He tapped his glass with hers again, prodding her to take another drink.

"How do you know those women?"

"They're friends of Tommy's."

"Do you know *all* these people?"

"Not everyone. I know some of the people here through Tommy."

"I don't see him. Is Tommy coming?"

"He said he'd be making the rounds. Maybe he'll show later. Finish your drink and let's dance."

With the midnight hour moments away, Butch ordered more drinks. A tuxedoed man grabbed the microphone and counted down to the stroke of midnight. Amidst cheering and shouts of, "Happy New Year," the Beechers embraced and kissed as the saxophonist heightened sentiments with a rendition of "Auld Lang Syne." Tuxedo man returned to the microphone.

"And now, here to help us start out the new year with a bang, all the way from Chicago, let's hear it for *Miss Baby New Year!*"

A statuesque woman entered wearing a red velvet dressing gown with a white feathered headdress. She launched into a choreographed burlesque performance. Her gown eventually gave way to a sparkling white corset and ended with her clad in nothing more than red sequin pasties and fringed undies. Men howled. Butch was mesmerized. Ladies applauded; Marie included.

"I see it didn't take long for you to forget about Temptress Greta," Marie remarked. "You don't know her, too, do you?"

"Not yet." He winked, hugged his bride and kissed her forehead. "How about another drink?"

"Oh, no, no, no, Carroll. Anymore and I'm going to be sick. Please. Let's go home."

Later that morning, Marie dragged herself to the kitchen, where Dorothy sat with baby Carol on her lap.

"Ugh. Good morning, sis. I'm sorry to sleep so late." Marie took Carol into her arms.

"You must have had quite a night. I can't wait to hear about the Ritz."

"I don't feel up to getting into it right now. We went downtown after the movie. It was the wildest thing I've ever seen. And the women he knows. Oh, my God."

"What! Who? What happened?"

"Really, I'm too hungover to talk about it. Some other time."

"Is everything alright?"

"Yes, it's just, the people he knows. It makes me wonder sometimes."

"Did he do something wrong?"

"No, not really."

"Do you trust him?"

Marie hesitated. "Yes, except when he's zozzled."

A car horn sounded outside. It was John's playful "Shave and a Haircut Song" horn blow . . . HONK-HA-HA-HONK-HONK. HONK-HONK.

"Father's here. Let's talk some more when you're feeling better."

Dorothy drove off with their father. Marie lingered in the kitchen with Carol, a cup of coffee and uneasy thoughts of the two babes surprisingly familiar with her man.

10.

MARGIE AND YET

M arie absolutely loved going to theaters to see vaudeville acts and movies. A favorite memory she talked of with her girls as they were growing up was attending one of the grand opening shows at Milwaukee's Oriental Theatre in 1927. Located on North Farwell Avenue, the Oriental was touted as one of America's greatest new picture palaces. Marie read about it and couldn't wait to see for herself. Amazingly, nine decades later, you can still see a movie at the Oriental and its ambitious design, as described in this excerpt from the theatre's website:

Designed to feel like a "temple of Oriental art," the Oriental Theatre was conceived of by the Milwaukee architecture firm Dick & Bauer and constructed by Saxe Amusement Enterprises in 1927. With design elements borrowed from Indian, Moorish, Islamic, and Byzantine architectural styles, the Oriental Theatre's eccentric, East Indian-inspired aesthetic resulted in 2,000 yards of lush textiles, faux teakwood ceiling timbers, intricate tile floors, Hindu-style pillars, onion-domed minarets, a porcelain-paneled entrance, and a stately terra cotta balustrade atop the theater roof.

In addition to these East Indian architectural features, guests
of the Oriental will find a pastiche of design elements that
contribute to the theater's extravagant ambience:

Three 8-foot chandeliers hang from the ceiling. Eight porcelain lions don
the staircase to the balcony. Numerous hand-painted murals of the Taj
Mahal and other giants of Eastern architecture line the walls. Countless
mythological creatures can be found in the plasterwork. Hundreds of
elephants are hidden throughout the interior. And enormous Buddha-
like figures with bright green eyes live inside decorative bays in the
main theater, keeping watch over moviegoers. Actress Greta Garbo
referred to it as "the last word in motion picture theaters."

"It was such a dreamy night," Marie recalled years later.
"Everyone was so amazed at the décor in the lobby and inside the
theatre. It was hard to stop looking at it all once the entertainment
started." Another feature of special interest for Marie was the
impressive pipe organ to the right of the stage. Its loud, rich tones
amplified the huge room's enchanting ambience. "Of course,
watching the man playing it, I couldn't help picturing my father
on the bench." At the time, it was said to be the largest theater
organ in the United States and third largest in the world. "There
was a stage act with dancing and an orchestra before the movie,"
Marie continued. "After they performed, the organist played a John
Philip Sousa medley. He finished with the 'Liberty Bell March' and
had all of us clapping along to the beat. It was all so festive; I had
a hard time settling down for the movie. Afterward, we went next
door to a place called Bensinger's. The Oriental and Bensinger's
were built where Farwell Station used to be, a big barn for horses
and streetcars. It was one of my most special nights and the funny
thing is, I don't remember much about the movie (*Naughty But*
Nice). I'll never forget it. Those were the good times."

Butch had hoped to take Marie out for another New Year's Eve night on the town, but she was not feeling well. In spite Butch's coaxing, it was not to be.

"I'll get on the blower and tell Dot not to come over," Marie offered. "If you want to go out, go ahead. Have a good time. Just don't get into any trouble." She knew she was better off with him out and happy, rather than sulking at home.

"I'm going to try to get home in time to be with you at midnight," Butch said, as he gave his wife a peck on the cheek. He headed out, dressed impeccably, as always.

Knowing how much her husband enjoyed having a good time, Marie had little faith in seeing him again before the next year. Unable to sleep, she passed the time with a book until she heard him return seven hours later, just after 3:00 a.m.

"You're up," he said, seeing her upright with a lamp on. "Sorry, I tried to get back sooner, but you know how it goes."

"Well, you had to know I was worried."

"You never have to worry about me, I know how to take care of myself."

"I know you can take care of yourself; I'm worried about who else might be trying to take care of you."

"Well, I'm here now, so you don't have to worry anymore," he answered dismissively.

The king of the castle had spoken. His tone signaled the end of discussion. Marie opted to surrender. She had learned by now, angering him after drinking could be dangerous.

By the end of January, Marie's suspicions were confirmed. She was pregnant again. Her happiness over the prospect of another baby was tempered in late March by news of a raid by federal prohibition agents.

"There was a raid at that hotel we were at for New Year's Eve," she told Butch while handing him the latest *Milwaukee Journal*.

"I heard."

"I'm worried about the men arrested. I hope they don't know you or Tommy."

"Not me. That's for sure. I was there just that one time with you. There's nothing to worry about."

Three months later, Marie struck up the same conversation, this time over a raid in the news at the St. Charles Hotel near City Hall.

Butch had the same offhanded response. "You worry too much. I don't even work with Tommy that much anymore."

"How would I know? You never want to talk about how you spend your time."

"That's because you like to get into every little detail. I don't."

"I think I have a right to know. We're going to have another mouth to feed soon. I need to know we're going to be okay financially."

"We will be, goddammit. I know what I'm doing. Quit worrying already."

———————————

On Saturday, August 18, Marie gave birth to Margaret Agnes Beecher in the same delivery room where her sister Carol had come into the world at Mount Sinai Hospital. By year's end, the Beecher's moved a short distance to another upper flat on North 31st Street. Perhaps they needed more room. Enough space for little Margie and Marie's growing uncertainty.

11.

HELEN

Bearcat: 1920s slang for a hot-blooded or fiery woman.

Marie suspected her Butch was seeing other women. In her wildest dreams, though, she could never have imagined his relatively innocent acquaintance with a bearcat who traveled four-hundred miles south, from her lair in Superior, Wisconsin, to take a big bite out of Milwaukee.

Her name was Helen Cromwell. Born in Indiana in 1886, she had made a living *pleasing* men from New York to San Francisco. In early 1920, buxom Helen came to Chicago, where she made fast friends with the city's mobster royalty. Her history prior to crossing paths with my grandfather is worthy of review.

By sheer happenstance, Helen started at the top. Her husband, Bob, accepted a dinner invitation from a new friend named James "Big Jim" Colisimo. Big Jim grew up in a South Side slum and rose to become boss of Chicago's South Side underworld. During their dinner, Big Jim introduced Helen to Johnny Torrio, a top Colisimo lieutenant and enforcer hailing from New York City. It was through Torrio that Helen first met Al Capone, another New York City transplant who followed Johnny to Chicago, now known as *Murder City*, in a quest for money and power.

Colisimo was assassinated in May 1920, most likely on orders from Torrio. Turf disputes between North and South Side mobsters escalated in a life-or-death power struggle over the next few years. Helen's husband, who had no mob involvement, died in 1923 from lung damage suffered during World War I in Europe. Capone averted an ambush. Torrio was shot twice and survived. He'd had enough and moved to spend the rest of his life in Italy. With Torrio's departure, Helen's friend, Al Capone, assumed control of the entire south side syndicate by late 1925. In October 1926, Capone had North Side mob boss Hymie Weiss killed, giving Al control over all organized crime in Chicago.

By that same time, Helen wanted to be an independent Madam with a *house* of her own. It was Capone who suggested Superior, Wisconsin, as an ideal place for Helen to ply her trade. He was right. In a year's time, she became the most prolific madam to ever *serve* the men in the mining industry there. Yet, Helen missed the bustle of the big city and once again, found herself in search of a new destination. When she eyeballed Milwaukee for the first time in 1927, she knew she had found the perfect place to finally settle down for good. In her 1966 autobiography, Helen described her new hometown:

> *Milwaukee in the late 1920s was a town of unblushing brawny vice rammed through with scents of European cooking, cheap perfume and workers' sweat. The rumbling, guttural accents of Germans, Dutchmen and Poles mingled with the silky Italian tones and were kneaded with bubbly sounds of sex to produce a symphony all its own. The city's gentry tried to mislead themselves into thinking of Milwaukee as fragile and culturally dainty, but it was a strong as an American buffalo.*

The bearcat from Superior spent a few days sniffing out neighborhoods to make her den. When she laid eyes on the Saint

Paul Street area, it's gritty feel instinctively appealed to her. She entered a plain, 30x65 foot building at 1806 St. Paul Avenue. Originally a four-room house, it was a bar turned Prohibition soda shop and a poorly hidden one at that, having been pinched several times by Milwaukee. There was no furnace, just a coal stove in the main room. Though neglected and in need of work, Helen saw it had affordable potential.

She went right up to the man behind the bar. "I'll give you three hundred dollars for the place."

"You're kidding. You actually want to buy this place?" he replied.

"That's what I said. I got three hundred bucks' cash on me right now. Deal?"

He didn't hesitate for a second. "You got a deal, lady." She gave him the money. He threw off his apron and waltzed out the door.

The next day, Schlitz Realty Company switched the property's lease to Helen's name. She scouted other speakeasies, both day and night, to gauge her competition. She hired cleaning women and repairmen, sprucing up the joint to her specifications. After learning the MPD's Moral Squad started their work at 9:00 p.m., Helen knew she would be greatly reducing her chances of getting caught by setting her hours from 9:00 a.m. to 9:00 p.m. Three weeks later, the madam extraordinaire opened the restaurant speakeasy. There was no sign. It simply became known as Helen's Place. In the coming years, it became known as the *Sunflower Inn*.

Butch's mother Margaret now lived on North 25th Street. Once he found Helen's place, he never visited one woman without visiting the other. Like the rest of Helen's growing clientele, Butch was captivated by her tales of travelling the country and all the interesting people she met, especially the Chicago mobsters only ninety miles to the south.

As if forbidden alcohol and bawdy tales weren't sensational

enough, it was the salt in her blistering tongue that earned the nickname that would come to attract curious Milwaukee visitors from across the country – *Dirty Helen.*

"Dirty Helen" Cromwell – photographer and date unknown

———————————

Earlier in 1928, Tommy got word of Dirty Helen's arrival. He tried unsuccessfully to become her alcohol supplier but told Butch, "You've got to go there for a drink and meet this woman for yourself. She's goddamn unbelievable."

He did. With regularity.

A week after Baby Margie was born, Butch strolled into Helen's place on a Sunday morning.

"Butch! You beautiful son-of-a-bitch, how the hell are ya?"

Helen bellowed from behind the bar. Handsome Butch was among her favorite new regulars.

"Never better, Hel . . ." his voice halted at the sight of the huge framed painting of a shapely naked woman on the wall behind Helen. "Look at the chassis on her. How are you today?"

"It just screwing-eh started, so I'd say perfect, so far. What'll ya' have?"

"House of Lords. After all, it's His day."

Helen laughed. "Now you're talking. That's my Lord's Day special every damn Sunday."

"What's with the painting?"

"Found it at a government auction. Used to hang in the juice joint at the Old Grove Hotel before the bulls shut it down. She cost me dearly, but when I saw her, I knew she belonged with me.

"Oh, it belongs, alright," Butch acknowledged.

"So, I'll ask you again, big guy. How the hell are you?"

"Good enough. Thought I'd stop for a pop or two before going to my mother's."

"How's she doing?" Helen asked as she poured shots of House of Lords whiskey into two glasses.

"The usual. Still busting my chops about joining the police force."

Helen laughed. "Really? You want to be a cop?"

"I did when I was a kid. She doesn't like what I do."

"Hell, does she even know what you do?"

"I don't know. She makes me feel like she does."

"Ha! You dumb son-of-a-bitch, that's what mothers do." Helen pushed one glass toward him and raising the other. "You're a good kid, Butchie. Here's to ya!"

"Prost!" Butch toasted back.

"Speaking of kids, we just had our second. Another girl. Named her Margaret, after my mother."

"No kidding? Well, good for you and the missus." Helen raised her glass for another sip and toast. "What's your first one's name?"

"Carol. Can I let you in on a secret?" Butch pushed his glass forward for Helen to pour another shot. "She's named after me."

"For Christ's sake, you named her Butch?"

Butch chuckled. "My real name's Carroll, with two R's and two L's."

"Well, here's to little Carol, big Carroll!" Helen toasted again, finishing her first shot while Butch downed his second.

"You know, you shouldn't have told me that, *CARROLL*. I'm going to have a screwin'-eh good time calling you by your girl name from now on."

He smiled, shook his head and looked down, regretting he trusted her with his birth name. As if he hadn't had enough teasing about it in his life.

"I'm just pulling your damn leg, Butch. I'm glad you're a daddy. You be a damn good one now, you hear me? Don't ever turn your back on your daughter, like my daddy did to me."

"Me? Never. Sorry to hear."

"Well, he wasn't the worst when I was a girl." She poured herself another shot. "But when I was 19, I married a man he hated, and he wouldn't speak to me again. Damnedest thing is though, the guy wound up cheating on me, so I guess my old man knew the guy was a weasel. Still wouldn't talk to me though. Anyway, makes me think about the cheating louse and bitch he slept with. Went up the stairs to her place and damn near scratched her eyes out. Left her face bloody. How's that for a happy ending?"

She ended her tale with a laugh. Once again, Butch stood speechless and shaking his head, in awe of the lady whose repartee was unlike any woman he had ever met.

Her attention shifted as two sailors walked in. "What can I do ya' for, boys?"

"We heard about your place," said the shorter of the two men. "Some mates of ours were here last week. Heard you have some ladies' upstairs that can show us a good time."

"Sure, I remember your mates. They were dimmer than a busted lighthouse, so I tossed those greenhorns out on their ear!"

Two sailors never looked so surprised.

"I'm just messing with ya' boys," Helen cackled. "Sorry, I ain't got pussy upstairs at this very moment. They'll be here, high noon."

"That's okay," the shorter of the two sailors replied. "We came up from Waukegan for the day. We're headed down to the Lakefront at noon. I'm not sure if we'll make it back later. What other days do you have ladies up there?"

"Oh, I got the best *pro skirt* damn near every screwin'-eh day of the week. You can pluck Rose on Tuesdays and Hazel on Hump Day. Friday's our payday special; I got Fanny and Franny. Give 'em each an extra fin and they'll do ya' at the same time. She looked at Butch, inviting him to nod along with her salacious repartee.

Her uniformed audience of two couldn't believe what they were hearing.

"Saturdays, well, that might be out of the price range for a couple of Waukegan Jack Tars. High rollers pay big sugar for top-shelf dames on Saturday. Most everybody knows that by now. Some local hicks think they can dick around with me on price. I tell 'em to blow, and if they don't get their ass in gear, I yell, 'Throw the bum out!' My regs give 'em the bums rush for me. It's screwin'-eh hilarious!"

Dumbfounded, the two sailors, mouths agape, stared back at Helen.

"You got your mouths open like you're used to having dicks in 'em."

The sailors looked at each other and howled with nervous

laughter. Shortie the Sailor spoke up again. "Thank you, ma'am. If I had the money, I'd be back every day, if I could."

His mate chimed in. "We're gonna shove off for today, but we'll be back."

"Fair enough, then. Thanks for giving us a look-see." As the young men headed out, she added, "Do me a favor. Tell all those swabs about my upstairs menu. Tell 'em to ask for Helen. That's me."

They laughed again and waved as they went out the door.

"I've gotta shove off, too," announced Butch as he pulled out his wallet to pay for his drinks.

"Hey, before you go, I wanted to tell you. You know, your man, Tommy, the one who wanted to sell me hooch? Word is, he's been pestering some people in Brookfield to buy from him. Next time you see him, you better tell him to back off. I know the fellas who have things covered there. They're the kind that'll rub out the competition."

"Thanks, Helen, I'll let him know. Is it your pal, Capone? I hear he's got a big house out in Brookfield."

"You heard right. I hear he stays there now and then. But it ain't Al's toes your man is stepping on. I won't say whose toes they are."

"Do you know if Al ever goes to Sam Pick's joint out there?"

"As a matter of fact, he does. You know Sam?"

"Yep. He used to get some of his hooch from us. Sam's a pal. I still go there to relax, if you get my drift."

She clapped her hands with a wiping motion and held her hands up, as if to say, mum's the word.

Butch winked and headed for the door.

"If you run into Al out there, say hello to him for me."

He waved without turning around and disappeared out the door.

12.

CRASHING

That very next morning, Butch passed on the warning. Tommy Boy took umbrage.

"I've been to a bunch of spots out there. I'm not leanin' on anyone. I'm not crowdin' anyone. Who was it?"

"She didn't say. I didn't ask. I think it's somebody big."

"Well, it can't be Pick. Since he dropped us at the club last year, he's got me delivering to that fancy new house of his on the Avenue. The son-of-a-bitch even has a speakeasy in his basement with a tunnel to a house across the street," he said of the residence that is known today as Brumder Mansion at North 31st Street and Wisconsin Avenue. "I've talked to him. We're jake."

"You're missing the point. It's nobody running a speak. It's a competitor. A dangerous one."

"So, what? I just give up my customers there? I've been workin' that area for years."

"Then keep the ones you can really trust. Otherwise, stay the hell out of there."

"Hey, I'm no pushover. Nobody tells me to stay out of town!"

"Look, cowboy, I'm telling you, Helen lived in Chicago. She's tight with Capone. If it's one of these Chicago boys, they'll put you down. You wanna be stupid, go ahead. It's your funeral."

"You're tellin' me what to do now?"

"Nope."

Tommy unfurled one side of his jacket to reveal the gun tucked in his belt. "Then, we do business where we want, when we want, and we wear iron to back it up." He leaned in with a finger poke to Butch's chest, eyes ablaze.

"Easy for you to say. I got a wife and kids. Tell you what, you do all the deliveries. I'll do pickup runs." By this time, they were getting Wisconsin-made booze from a distillery in Monroe and moonshiners in the *Holyland*, a rural area east of Fond du Lac where enterprising German-Catholic farmers lived by their own rules when it came to alcohol.

"So, you're a piker now. Gone soft from makin' babies, is that it?"

"Cheese the gat, you're out of control."

"Make me."

Butch put him down with a mighty backhand swing of *northpaw* knuckles. "Do it all yourself then, you dumb bastard. I'm out." He stepped off with Tommy still down, holding his right cheek.

A few days later, the boys patched things up, at least for a while. Tommy agreed to Butch's offer to do pickups until summer 1929, when Tommy told Butch he didn't need him anymore. Butch took a job delivering newspapers for the Milwaukee Journal Company.

———————————

Things were looking up for Marie. She was quite pleased that Butch had predictable work hours for the first time. More than that, there were no more cryptic calls between her man and Tommy.

To Marie's further delight, the month of October delivered another milestone for the family of Leicht. Dorothy married Jerome "Jerry" Weirich. Marie returned the favor of standing as

Maid of Honor for her sister in a ceremony that took place on Thursday the 24th, also Dorothy's birthday.

On the same day that joy peaked for Marie and her loved ones, the stock market dropped 11 percent of its entire value at the Wall Street stock exchange in New York City. Three trading days later, a frenzy of panic selling exploded at the opening bell. Bedlam ensued on the trading floor and in the streets outside the stock exchange. Combined with the London stock market crash a month earlier, Tuesday October 29 marked the Great Crash of '29 on New York's Wall Street stock exchange. Locally, the bold-face headline of that evening's *Milwaukee Journal* read:

S.S. Wisconsin Sunk – 10 Dead
Boat Goes Down Near Kenosha, 63 Rescued

Stock market turmoil appeared as the second story on the front page, headlined: **16 Million Share Day Swamps Market.**

With such a tragic main headline, it's likely that few Milwaukeeans at the time understood the long-term significance of the second story. In fact, the next day's *Journal* headline eased concerns, at least in the near-term: **General Rally Allays Market Hysteria.**

Then came Halloween night. Children out and about for trick-or-treat had yet to become a custom. Other than sporadic pranks of vandalism by rowdy teenagers, it was just another night. That is, until the telephone rang in the Beecher residence after Marie put her little girls to bed. Marie went to the kitchen and picked up the phone to answer, wondering if it could be Butch, who hadn't returned home from work.

It wasn't Butch. It was Betty. *Brookfield Betty.*

"Hello, I need to talk with Butch please."

"Who is this?"

"Who are you? I want to talk with Butch."

"I'm his wife. Who are you and why are you calling?"

"If you must know, I'm Betty. He knows who I am."

"If *you* must know, *Betty*, he's not home right now."

"Well, he needs to come see me. I miss him. Would you let him know, sweetie?"

"Oh, I'll let him know, alright." Marie slammed her phone's earpiece back onto its cradle.

She melted into a kitchen chair, sautéed by confirmed suspicion. Her spirit liquified to the rhythm of twelve-hundred second-hand ticks. Then, came the sounds of his footsteps and the back door opening. Marie looked up at him with tear-filled eyes.

"Your lady friend called and asked for you."

"What?"

"Your girlfriend, Betty, called on the phone for you."

"What are you talking about?"

"Oh, you know exactly who I'm talking about."

"No, I don't," he claimed, with the telltale deceit of a kid caught with a hand in the cookie jar.

"Yes, you do. I can tell. It was Betty. She misses you."

"If it's who I think it is, she's just a booze hound friend of Tommy's."

Marie stood. "Really, Butch? How could you?"

"Oh, c'mon, Ree? She's crazier than a weasel in heat."

"You promised me. You said you would never break my heart." She turned and went to their bedroom.

He took off his coat and hat, knowing he'd been had by Tommy. His old pal must have given Betty his phone number.

13.

MOTHER'S NATURE

A charade of holiday happiness. After the Beechers hosted relatives for Thanksgiving and Christmas, the jig was up. Ailing Margaret told her son she needed him at her apartment the next morning. When he arrived, Margaret Clancy-Beecher lowered the boom.

"Alright, Carroll. I know something's wrong. What's going on?"

Hearing his formal name and feeling the pierce of her eyes was bad enough. Seated in view behind her, the eyes of his Grandmother Mary delivered the full double-whammy. "What do you mean?" he asked, wondering which indiscretion she had discovered.

"Something's wrong between you and Marie. No question about it. I can tell. What's going on?" Margaret knew her son. His penchant for gin joints and women. She sensed the pain of betrayal beneath Marie's mask. Only one person in the world could squeeze some truth out of him Standing face-to-face with that person, Butch had to come clean.

"Marie thinks I've been seeing another woman."

"And what would give her that idea?"

"Some dame called the house a while back. She's just a booze hound friend of Tommy's that got the wrong idea about me."

"My boy, I can read you like a book. If you think your wife can't read you, too, you're just foolin' yourself."

He stood in silence, unable to look her in the eye.

"What the hell is the matter with you? When you were a boy, you wanted to be a policeman. Now you're grown up and still acting like a boy, like a hooligan. What would your father think?"

Butch grimaced, still unable to look at her.

His mother stepped closer to chide with a wag of an arthritic forefinger. "You straighten up and I mean it. You're a father now; once you're a father, that's it!" she declared, flinging her wag hand sideways. Waving off hanky-panky for good. "You have a wonderful wife. I've held your wonderful girls in my arms, like I held *you*. That's your purpose, not screwing around. Hold *them*! Carry *them*!"

Her chastened son looked at her and nodded.

"You promise me right now, you're going to keep your nose fixed on legitimate work, Carroll August. Carroll means warrior. Promise me you're going to be a warrior for good."

Her son nodded again.

"Let me hear ya say it. Promise!"

"Yes, I promise," Butch replied, his tone mixed with guilt and the sting of a verbal thrashing he knew he deserved.

Margaret turned her back on him, retiring to her room with tears in her eyes. Cold-shouldered by his own mother, Butch left in silence to return home. Marie continued to barely acknowledge his presence. Her greatest weapon was the silent treatment. It echoed in his conscience with deafening effectiveness.

———————

1930. It was the first Unhappy New Year Butch and Marie had experienced together. Though Milwaukee had 94 movie theaters by the end of the Roaring '20s, Marie had no interest in going out for a New Year's Eve show, at least not with her husband.

January 4. Another devastating phone call came to the Beecher residence.

Butch's mother had died in her sleep at the age of 52. His grandmother Mary found her in bed after she'd gotten up that morning and didn't see Margaret in the kitchen.

Margaret Clancy Beecher was buried next to her husband, August, in the family plot at Calvary Cemetery. Mary moved to live with her granddaughter, Butch's sister Minette.

Ironically, it was Margaret's death that led to some ice melting between her son and Marie, who was seven when her own mother died. If anyone understood the loss of a mother, it was Marie. To her credit, she supported Butch during his mother's loss as if nothing had happened between them.

14.

BLACK TO BLUE

Promise. The last word Margaret spoke to her son. Grief for loved ones is inescapable. When coupled with genuine remorse, it can be transformational. If Margaret knew her time was short, her final exhortation cemented her place in Irish heaven, the Gaelic *Queen of Hearts*.

Humbled, Butch sought counsel, but instead of a priest, he went to Helen for a shot of courage and a dose of straight-forward advice.

"Hey, Butchie boy, how the hell are you doing?"

"Not too good." He answered and paused. "My mother died."

"Oh, no. God, I'm real sorry to hear, Butch."

He nodded to thank her.

"Your ma was Irish, right? Lemme pour you an Old Fitz (Fitzgerald). On the house."

"Thanks, Helen."

She poured a generous shot and watched him sip, rather than downing it instantly. "How'd she die, if you don't mind my asking?"

"In her sleep. She hadn't been feeling well for a while."

"The best way to go, but I know me saying that won't make you feel any better about it."

He nodded again. With only two other gents conversing over drinks, he seized the moment.

"You mind giving me some advice?"

"Hell, that's what I do, especially for fellas who don't ask for it but need it."

"Ma always wanted me to be a policeman. You think I could be a cop?"

"Doesn't matter what I think. What do you think?"

"I thought about it growing up. Decided it wasn't for me when Prohibition came along. There's no way I could give someone a hard time for drinking."

"I get that. You do know the City Council voted to stop enforcement. The state, too. The boys in blue don't have to play that game anymore. Just the goddamn Feds."

"I'm aware."

"How are you makin' a living these days?"

"The *Milwaukee Journal*. Delivery driver."

"Heck, the blue boys need drivers, too. The other thing is, the economy's in the crapper. A city job's a good thing to have. Have you cranked out any more kids?"

"Nope, still just the two."

"Well, you never know. You might. You got a wife and family. You know damn well how proud they'd be if you're one of Milwaukee's finest, just like your Ma would. That's my advice, kid. Now, how 'bout another drink?"

"No, but thanks, Helen. Trying to cut back, believe it or not."

"Now you're scarin' me, kid. Christ, be a cop. We'll still love ya'. Just don't stop drinking."

What Helen said about Wisconsin was true. Political leaders expressed the will of the people by rejecting Prohibition enforcement gained national attention. Even at the federal level, a leading enforcement official acknowledged that the drinking in the state's culture was sacrosanct:

"To the average American unacquainted with actual conditions therein, is commonly regarded as a Gibraltar of the wets, sort of a Utopia where everybody drinks their fill and John Barleycorn still holds forth in splendor. From the standpoint of actual votes and of present conditions, Wisconsin is undoubtedly a wet Commonwealth."

~Frank Buckley, Bureau of Prohibition

With reassurance from his *other mother*, his path to redemption was clear. Butch applied at the Milwaukee Police Department (MPD). The two-page application form contained a section for listing the names of five character references. He listed his father-in-law, John, a pillar of integrity. The other men he listed were current members of the force. All were speakeasy friendlies from bootlegging days. There were no guarantees. He would have to bide his time.

It was his year of making amends and pursuing dreams. He was a fine baseball pitcher, good enough, he felt, to partake in an open tryout held by the Milwaukee Brewers minor professional baseball team at Athletic Field on 8th and Chambers Streets. Afterward, he joked about the experience and the presence of Otto Borchert, the Brewers flamboyant owner.

"I got a whiff of being a professional pitcher. It was the smell of Otto Borchert's cigar when he walked right past me."

A more attainable dream did come true. After renting four different flats in five years, the Beechers occupied an entire house of their own, a two-story rental at 1634 North 35th Street. As the year passed, Butch kept the embers of his application alive. After several hiring office check-ins and put-in-a-good-word-for-me glad-handing, the wheels finally turned in his favor.

On April 8, 1931, Carroll Beecher officially joined the Milwaukee Police Department. He was assigned Badge Number 1059. In the hereafter, Margaret's Irish eyes were smiling.

Marie turned 27, two days later on Friday, April 10. The next day, Dorothy came to the Beecher house for nanny time with nieces Carol and Margie. It seemed like forever since Butch had taken Marie out on the town. They returned to Marie's favorite, the Oriental Theatre, to see *Chasing Rainbows.* a jaunty, romantic musical starring Charles King, Bessie Love, and featuring vaudeville comic, Jack Benny, in his first film role. The movie also introduced the song that went on to become an anthem for Americans coping with the prolonged economic downturn that would come to be known as, "The Great Depression:"

> *Happy days are here again*
> *The skies above are clear again*
> *Let us sing a song of cheer again*
> *Happy days are here again.*

The night out had its intended effect. Marie forgave him and swooned the first time she saw him in uniform. Privately, concern for his safety surpassed her fear of his dormant infidelity. After weeks of training at the Milwaukee Police Academy, he was assigned to District 5 as a third shift patrol officer, otherwise known as graveyard-shift beat cop. Hours of duty were from midnight to 8 a.m. His first year of duty was on a probationary basis. A field service officer worked closely with him during his first three months, and then Butch's autonomy gradually increased during his subsequent months of probation status. A night owl by nature, Butch's adjustment was relatively easy. Sometimes he slept a bit in the afternoon. Other times he'd catch an hour or two of shut eye before heading in to work.

On the domestic front, Marie enjoyed her new family structure. Carol and Margie now saw their father at consistent intervals and much more per day than ever. He'd rarely talked about work with Marie in the past. Doing police work did nothing to change that. As wives will do, she wanted to hear the details of his shift, to understand what her husband was experiencing. As men tend to do, he didn't want to rehash the who, what, when, where, and why of experiences she wouldn't understand, the rough-and-tumble of making a living in a man's world. It was his wall of independence and, in another sense, his way of protecting her. Butch's maturing sense of responsibility would have to be enough. Emotional connection was for women. It was the best that most housewives in that era could hope for.

15.

GROWING PAINS

Times were tough for seemingly everyone at the start of 1932. National unemployment was at 25 percent. Yet, in the first two years of the Great Depression, the diversity of Milwaukee's industries helped stave off the significant job loss occurring in other major cities. So much so, that the city was dubbed, the "Milwaukee Miracle."

That changed dramatically as 1932 unfolded. Milwaukee experienced massive layoffs. By year's end, the number of wage earners in the city had dropped by nearly two-thirds since the Depression's onset. Poverty became rampant as many families lost their homes and went hungry. The lucky ones were those who found family or friends willing to take them in. Cramped living quarters were the norm. The least fortunate of the homeless and destitute in Milwaukee built small shanties and shacks in Estabrook Park along the Milwaukee River. Scraps of lumber, tin, brick, cardboard, canvas or tarpaper were used to create makeshift structures for protection from the elements. Communities of homeless people that cropped up across the country became known as "Hoovervilles." The derisive term bore the name of President Herbert Hoover, the man who many felt was to blame for the onset of the Great Depression. In November, voters voiced their frustrations by ousting President

Hoover in favor of the Democratic Governor of the State of New York, Franklin Roosevelt.

The Beechers weathered the economic storm. With so many people desperate for food and shelter, the city juggled their budget to ensure the MPD stayed fully funded. Order had to be maintained to prevent crime and looting. As Mayor Daniel Hoan put it, "A business may quit, your city can't." Butch continued to work third shift and periodic double shifts, as he had in 1931.

Patrolman Beecher. Wife Marie. 1932
(Photos by Marie's brother-in-law Jerome Weirich, Sr.)

Part of the experience of being a policeman's wife is learning to coexist with inherent danger her husband faces. A tragic example of that reality happened earlier that year. Patrolman

Richard Zingler was shot in the chest on February 7 by one of three young men attempting to rob an apartment superintendent of rent money. Zingler died the next day, leaving behind a wife and six-year-old son.

For Marie, the disturbing nature of the event was doubled by the reality that the daytime shooting had occurred six blocks away. When Marie realized she was pregnant four months later, she pushed to relocate. "I understand you have an attachment to this area," she told Butch. "I'm just not comfortable here anymore since the shooting. I don't want Carol and Margie out walking to school here. Plus, we're going to need more room. I really want to see what's available in that new Garden Homes neighborhood."

"If we can afford it, fine with me."

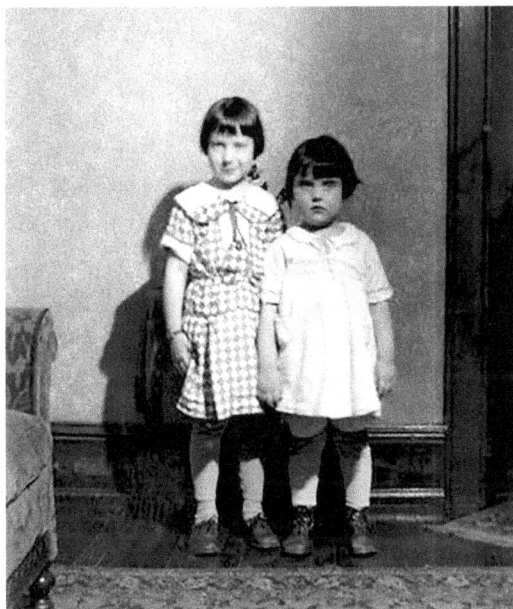

My mother, Carol (age 5), with her sister, Margie (age 3)
(Photo by Jerome Weirich, Sr.)

The Garden Homes neighborhood had been developed a few years earlier through the first municipally sponsored housing project in the country. Butch and Marie took a drive to what had once been countryside. Four miles later, rows of newer homes came into view north of Capitol Drive.

"Turn left on 25th Street. That's where that new church and school are, the ones I heard about from father."

After turning, they saw Saint Agnes Catholic Parish to their left. Butch pulled to a stop.

"Oh, my, can't you just picture Carol starting school there in September?"

Butch said nothing. His raised brows and approving nod spoke for him.

Marie looked to the back seat where six-year-old Carol looked out the window behind her father. "Wouldn't that be a nice school to go to?"

Carol looked at her mother and shrugged.

Butch resumed driving and stopped again at the sight of a *For Rent* sign in front of 4139 North 25th Street. Marie clutched his shirt sleeve, unable to hide her excitement.

"Oh, my God, Butch. This is too good to be true. This is it!" She slid across the front seat, raising her left hand and peering back to count the number of houses to the school with her forefinger. "One, two, three, four, five, *six*. Six houses to the school, Butch! Six!"

Butch broke their lease on 35th Street, and, ten weeks later, Marie held Carol's hand while walking to school from their new home on North 25th Street. Marie loved her new surroundings, although the move put distance between her and her sisters. The tradeoff meant she would have to fend for herself during the remaining months of a pregnancy. On Monday December 19, Marie gave birth to another girl. She weighed nearly two pounds less at birth than her sisters.

Daughter number three was named Joan Rose Beecher.

———————————

*Let me assert my firm belief that the only
thing we have to fear is fear itself.*
~Franklin Delano Roosevelt

Newly elected President Franklin Roosevelt's stirring inaugural address in March 1933 offered hope and inspiration to the millions of Americans listening through the magic of radio.

No one took it to heart more than Marie. She'd had her hands full throughout the year. Baby Joan was sickly right from the start. Carol's grades in her first year of school were above average, but she struggled mightily with anxiety away from home. Margie suffered for weeks with a springtime bout of whooping cough. Polio cases were at near epidemic proportions nationwide.

Worry loomed constantly for Marie. Joanie was often colicky. On some days, her crying was non-stop. Marie could barely get her to take in food. At night, Joanie slept in short intervals and cried the rest of the time. Marie was a wreck from no sleep.

Butch also struggled with loss of sleep and patience. It may account for an outburst he had with a citizen on an August night, leading to placement of a formal reprimand in his permanent record. Unlike Marie, at least he had an escape. His new berth on the vaunted MPD baseball team was an ideal outlet. He could flash his baseball skills and drink with the boys afterward. Like most women at the time, Marie didn't drive. A Sunday visit to see family after Butch was available to drive following the baseball season afforded Marie a precious break from isolation.

Left to right: Carol, Margie, Marie, Joanie, Butch
(Sunday, October 8, 1933 – Photo by Jerome Weirich, Sr.)

In the spring of 1934, they moved again, this time to a house right behind theirs, at 4122 North 26th Street. Why they moved is unclear. Maybe for a better landlord or more space. One plausible reason is clear. Marie was pregnant again with another due date in mid-December.

Stress from the previous year moved right along with them. Joanie had constant health "problems." In the days following Butch's 29th birthday, he endured tense, nerve-racking extra shifts during the biggest outbreak of mob violence in the city's history, triggered from a strike by the AFL (American Federation of Labor) against the Milwaukee Electric Railway and Light Company. Striking workers were joined by hordes of frustrated unemployed young men, as violence escalated each night from June 26th through June 28th. Police used tear gas to disperse a mob of 12,000 at the Kinnickinnic Avenue streetcar barn on the south side. A mob of 10,000 rioted at the Fond du Lac Avenue barn on the north side and broke an estimate 100 windows. At one point, an eight-hour stoppage of streetcar service caused the worst traffic jams in city history. In total, one person died, 50 were injured, including 7 police patrolmen and detectives, and 97 were arrested. The company brought the strike to an end, giving workers a five to seven percent pay increase and agreeing to reinstate fired workers. Years later, Butch recalled the experience:

> I was assigned to crowd control on Fond du Lac Avenue. We wore helmets. We had our batons at port arms and parallel, pushing guys back. Most of them didn't come at us. The ones that did, we put down. I jabbed a few in the gut with my stick, whacked a few in the shin. We weren't trying to advance, just keep them contained. Mobs are scary. They get that crazed look in their eyes. It was bad, as bad as any experience in my time on the force.

Lest I forget a matter of note, the 21st Amendment to the Constitution had officially repealed Prohibition, back on December 5, 1933. Butch began to make legal morning tavern stops with increasing regularity as 1934 rolled by. If it helped him to cope, it didn't work in early November, when he failed to obey orders from a superior officer. Butch later apologized but the damage was done. Another formal reprimand was placed on his permanent record. Disciplinary rules for a second offense resulted in being docked two days' pay. After the incident, Butch requested reassignment to an earlier shift. He also requested a transfer to a first-shift job in the Bureau of Investigation at downtown headquarters. His submittal would be delayed one year as a consequence of his rule violation.

In a month, Marie was due to have her fourth baby. She hoped for a son, as did Butch.

"Maybe you'll finally have your 'Danny Boy,'" Marie mused, knowing how sentimental Butch got when hearing the classic Irish ballad.

"When you have him, I'll sing it for you, first thing."

December was a repeat of baby preparations two years earlier. Carol and Margie had their bedroom. As she approached her second birthday, Joanie now had her own bedroom. Her crib in Mom and Dad's room was ready for baby number four.

On December 12, the newborn arrived. Sure enough – Marie had a boy.

He was named Daniel James Beecher. He was stillborn.

Both mother- and father-to-be were no strangers to tragedy, each having lost a parent and a sibling during childhood. Now they would have to bear the crushing loss of their much anticipated first son.

16.

THE GREAT DEPRESSION

The Toy Maker: What do you think of the wooden soldiers?
Santa Claus: They're nice but they're not what I ordered.
I ordered 600 soldiers one foot high.
Stannie Dum (Stan Laurel): Oh, I thought you said
100 soldiers six feet high.

Giggles wiggled out of the Beecher girls. Carol and Margie looked up at their father. They weren't sure if it was okay to laugh. Daddy flashed a reassuring smile. Butch took his two oldest girls to the Ritz to see the Laurel and Hardy comedy, *Babes in Toyland.*

It was Saturday; just three days after the girls came home from school to learn they would not have a baby brother after all. One week remained in their school semester. Carol was in 3rd Grade. Margie was in 1st Grade and, unlike her older sister, couldn't wait for each school day to arrive. They had missed school the previous day for Daniel's burial at Holy Cross, a cemetery within the Archdiocese of Milwaukee with an area designated for baby burials, at no charge to bereaved Catholic parents. The funny

Saturday matinee was a welcome respite and gave the girls a break from the gloom at home.

Strength to carry the family through Christmas would have to come from Butch. Marie could barely go through the motions each day. She rarely spoke. What little energy she had was focused on little Joanie, whose second birthday was overshadowed by grief.

"How is my little Joanie today?" Marie would ask, with a forced smile and heartbreak in her eyes. Joanie's frailty seemed the one thing that motivated Marie in her grief.

When Butch wasn't working, he fulfilled duty at home. No tavern stops. He drank at home. He made sure the girls did their homework and pitched in with chores. One day, he rewarded them with surprise gifts.

"It's a *Peter Cottontail* puzzle!" Marge exclaimed.

"Mine is called Blowing Bubbles," Carol said. It featured a scene of a little girl blowing bubbles in a flower garden.

America was experiencing a jigsaw puzzle craze. Toy manufacturers produced die-cut, cardboard jigsaw puzzles to meet demand for entertaining activities at prices families struggling through the Great Depression could afford.

Unfortunately, Daddy was beset by a puzzle he couldn't solve, nor could anyone else. His wife was in real trouble mentally. Butch spoke privately with father-in-law, John, when he visited in late April on Easter Sunday.

"She's just not coming around," Butch said. "She doesn't smile anymore, not even when she's around the kids."

"I've been doing a little reading about things like this. It's called reactive depression."

"I don't care what it's called. How do I get her to snap out of it?"

John nodded. "I keep in touch with Father Devlin. Remember? The priest who did your wedding. He's got as much experience with counseling as anyone in the world," John said of his longtime friend and former pastor at Gesu Church. "He might know how to deal with this kind of thing. I'll talk to him. I think he can help."

Two days later, Father Devlin paid a mid-afternoon visit to the Beecher house. Butch walked with his daughters to nearby Garden Homes Park, agreeing to return in an hour while the priest met privately with Marie.

"Marie, your father asked me talk with you about how you are doing. Losing a child is devastating. I won't say that I know how you feel, because I can't. I can't possibly know what it's like. Please, could you tell me about it?"

Marie sat expressionless. "I'm sorry, Father. I just can't talk about it."

"Well, could you just tell me what's on your mind? What do you think about when you wake up in the morning?

"Nothing. I worry about my baby, Joanie. She's sick a lot. She needs me."

"What about your other two girls. They still need you, too. Don't they?"

Marie paused and then nodded. No words came out. She closed her eyes. Her lips quivered. She covered her face with both hands.

"Can you tell me what Butch can do to help you? What your father and I can do to help you in some way?"

Still covering her face, she shook her head briefly.

"Is there anything you would like to tell me? You don't have to say anything right away. Just think about it. I will be quiet. You can speak when you're ready."

A minute or two passed. Marie slowly uncovered her face, wiping the wetness from her eyes. Father Devlin pulled his rosary out and prayed for her silently.

"I died," Marie said softy, looking down. "I died with Danny."

"I'm so sorry, my dear. I will pray for you. Would you like to pray a little along with me?

She said nothing. He resumed praying with his rosary, this time in a whispering tone. After another minute passed, Marie got up and walked slowly away to her bedroom.

Father Devlin waited for Butch to return and speak to him privately.

"I have to be honest with you, Butch. She really is in a deep melancholy. She said little, but confidentially, she did say she feels dead, that she died with her baby. She should be evaluated at County Hospital. They can give her a thorough exam and determine the best approach to help her. It's possible they may even admit her for extended treatment. You should be prepared for that possibility."

Butch thanked the priest for his help. Within twenty-four hours, he coordinated with John, Dorothy, and Agnes to make needed preparations to care for the children in their mother's absence.

The time came for Butch and John to inform Marie and take her to Milwaukee County General Hospital. In a matter of hours, she was admitted and placed in their facility for mental diseases. Treatment began with a ten-day period of hydrotherapy consisting of hot baths by day and sedatives at night. Each day, Marie was assisted by nurses into a hydrotherapy steam cabinet, basically a wooden box with a bench for the patient to sit on. Once the patient was seated, the nurses closed the upper panel of the chamber, producing the strange sight of the occupant's head protruding from the top of the chamber. Full body exposure to hot steam was believed to produce a calming effect upon the mind and central nervous system. On alternating afternoons, Marie was forced into a bathtub where she was made to lie until shortly before the 5 p.m. dinner hour. An attendant would cover her with a rubber sheet so that only her head wasn't under water. She was strapped in to restrict her movement and prevent her from getting out. Marie was surrounded by several other patients also receiving the same treatment. Bath water temperatures were machine controlled, maintaining a range from 92-99°F to avoid causing injury to the patient. Attendants were instructed to squelch attempts at conversation between patients on the theory that discussion might cause patients to lose focus on total relaxation of the mind. Visitors were prohibited during what turned out to be a four-week stay.

Her release was arranged for Sunday, May 26. Butch arrived to pick up his wife. When they arrived back to their 26th Street home, all of Marie's loved ones were there to welcome her – John and Agnes, Dorothy with her husband Jerome and their children – Mary, Jerome Jr. and one-year old, Walter. Above all, she was greeted by Marie's precious daughters. All three girls rushed to their mother's open arms, as she gushed with emotion.

"Oh, my beautiful girls! I missed you so much!"

"Mommy, Mommy!"

Marie and her daughters meshed in a four-way hug, releasing pent-up emotion in a cacophony of muffled crying, words and sniffles.

Butch made plans for the following Sunday. He picked up Agnes and brought her over to nanny the girls. He took Marie out to the nearby Ritz on Villard Avenue for a matinee showing of *The Little Colonel*, a *saccharine romp showcasing the song and dance talents of Hollywood's littlest starlet*, Shirley Temple, who co-starred with Lionel Barrymore. A highlight of the film, albeit a controversial one for the times, featured Shirley's famous staircase dance with black actor, Bill Robinson, who played a butler working in a southern plantation mansion after the Civil War, in the post-slavery culture of the Deep South. It was the first interracial dance pairing in Hollywood history. Most audiences found it delightful. Some felt it was an abomination, and, in the Deep South, many theater operators cut the scene out of the movie.

Butch leaned toward Marie and quietly said, "I think I know her."

"Who?"

"The colored woman, I think she worked at a place I used to delivery to," whispered Butch.

Marie replied with a puzzled look, and they continued to watch the movie.

Butch was awaiting the ending movie credits and saw the name – *Hattie McDaniel*. "It IS her!" Butch declared. "She's the heavy-set woman who played the house slave, Mammy."

"Are you putting me on? How could you know someone like her?"

"She worked at Club Madrid in Brookfield. Me and Tommy made deliveries there years ago. She waited on tables. A bathroom attendant, too, I think. Sam Pick still owns the joint. She talked him into letting her sing once. He made her a regular performer."

"How about that? You met her and now she's in the movies? She must be talented. Good for her."

After the movie, Butch took Marie to a nearby restaurant for a special early dinner treat. Initially, she balked at the idea.

"Oh no, I've got to get home to make supper for the kids."

"Agnes has it covered. No need to worry."

Marie allowed herself to savor a degree of attention from Butch that she hadn't experienced in a long time. She even indulged in a glass of wine, while Butch treated himself with Kentucky bourbon, a drinking man's treat that had become readily available again in Milwaukee's post-prohibition world. As they dined, Marie remarked about how adorable little Fritzi was, the little terrier that was Shirley's sidekick in the movie. Butch had just ordered his third bourbon and was on a benevolence roll.

"Would you like a dog like that?" he asked.

"Well, of course, I'd love to, but we can't afford a dog."

"Hell, yeah. Why not?" Butch replied.

Marie leaned forward with wide eyes.

"There's two pet shops on my beat. We'll take the girls there Saturday. Maybe they've got a Fritzi."

Her face lit up as bright as the Ritz marquee.

"Oh, Butch, that would be wonderful! Thank you so much." She jumped from her chair to kiss and hug him.

Sure enough, Saturday arrived, and the five Beechers went to a pet shop on Green Bay Avenue. Marie and the girls were mesmerized by a perky terrier pup. She was white with subtle spots in her coat and symmetrical tan marking around her eyes and ears. Butch paid the shop keeper, who prepared a box to carry their new pup in. The family's Ford Tudor Sedan was never filled with as much joy as it was on that afternoon ride home. Once they returned home, Carol and Margie fizzed with ideas for a name. Later that night when Butch left for work, Marie warmed to him at departure time in a way she hadn't in years. "You made the girls and me so happy today. Be safe out there, dear. Toodle-oo."

When the girls woke and came to the kitchen the next morning, before they sat, their mother caught their attention with a beaming grin and wide eyes.

"I've got the name." Her girls looked up at her, mouths agape. "Toodles!"

"Yes! Toodles! Toodles! Toodle-oo Toodles!" the girls squealed, jumping up and down in unanimous approval, energized by the sight of their mother announcing the name with huge grin, her arms and fingers outstretched at 10-and-2 like Minnie Mouse come to life.

Lightness returned to the Beecher household for the summer. Unfortunately, as autumn turned, Marie's buoyancy did, too. Toodle's presence could not forestall her return to the void. On school mornings, she barely spoke, focusing only on Joanie. Carol helped Margie get ready for school. They went out the door, wondering if their mother might be gone again soon. Joanie developed a viral infection in November that led to a double ear infection. The Saint Agnes School semester break started on December 20, a day after Joanie's third birthday. It seemed once her older girls were home on break with Joanie, Marie stopped getting up in the morning. After a bleak Christmas Day, Butch checked his wife back into the county sanitarium. A doctor familiar with Marie's case gave Butch his assessment.

"She is suffering from a form of regressive catatonia. I attributed her first treatment here to the depressive state that some women experience after a stillbirth. It's uncommon for a relapse this severe but not unheard of. We'll start with the same approach as her last treatment and see how she responds."

Marie's second stay lasted eight weeks. Family gathered again for a second "welcome back" day at the Beecher house, where she would now try to function with aid of Benzedrine pills. It was a pioneering decade in the relationship between the medical profession and an emerging pharmaceutical industry that urged psychiatrists, neurologist and general practitioners to prescribe amphetamines for certain conditions, including depression.

On May 24th, the same relatives returned to celebrate Carol's First Holy Communion. Knowing my mother, she probably disliked all the attention. Her guests must have been equally pleased with how well her mother appeared to be doing.

*My Mother's First Communion Day with her
grandfather John Leicht and Toodles*

*Marie and Carroll "Butch" Beecher on Carol's First Communion Day
(Photos by Jerome Weirich, Sr. – May 24, 1936)*

Normalcy continued for the Beechers through 1936. Optimism surged when Marie not only made it through the holidays but maintained through wintertime for the first time in three years. Dorothy continued to be her lone confidant. Her bond with Marie was as strong as ever. With three children each and drinking husbands who sometimes got physical, they had reasons to commiserate by phone regularly.

"I feel so badly for Carol lately," Marie confided.

"Why, what's wrong?"

"When the girls came home from school last week, Carol was crying. She wouldn't talk about it, but later Margie told me. Some of the kids are picking on her, calling her *fatty boom boom*."

"Oh, the poor thing. God, kids can be so cruel. Why didn't she tell you?"

"Well, I assumed because she was embarrassed, but Margie said Carol told her to not talk about it with me, that it would just make me sad again."

Dorothy was silent, perhaps at a loss for the right thing to say.

"God, it's all my fault. My girls are afraid to talk to me. Joanie is sick all the time. It never stops. I'm not a good mother."

"My God, Marie, don't say that. You know that's not true."

"It is. I think about it all the time. I'm always worried if I'm acting normal enough. My body doesn't feel right. My hands are shaking. Sometimes, I feel like I'm going crazy. I really do."

"You're going to be alright, Marie. Really, things will work out eventually. You just have to stay positive, sweetheart. You'll see."

Further insight came later that year, in a private kitchen moment while Dorothy hosted Thanksgiving.

"I hope you don't mind. I happened to mention to Father

last week about your skin problems. He said mother had chronic psoriasis. It's probably hereditary."

"Why would you do that? Don't talk about things like that with Father anymore. I'm sick of everyone knowing my problems."

"Of course, dear. I'm sorry. It just sort of came up when Father was over here. I got hiccups that wouldn't stop. He laughed about how mother would have hiccup spells. I started asking him more things about Mother, and it just came up."

"Did you tell him I'm losing my mind? Did mother have a problem with that, too?"

"No, of course not Marie and no you're not. Let's keep it fun. It's Thanksgiving. We have a lot to be thankful for."

Marie (left) wearing an apron with Dorothy and sons on Labor Day at Pewaukee Lake (Photo by Jerome Weirich Sr. – September 6, 1937)

1938. It began with Butch finally getting the desk job he'd been angling for. He was assigned to special duty on first shift at the Bureau of Identification downtown. Marie and the girls were glad his day was now in rhythm with theirs for the very first time.

Marie's hand tremors and weepiness became impossible for her girls to ignore.

"Mama's hands are shaking so bad, she can't sew," Margie said to her sisters. Her first Eucharist was in two weeks. She saw their mother's unsuccessful attempts to alter Carol's communion dress for her.

"I know," Carol said, shaking her head. "She's been shaking at breakfast every morning."

"She's talking funny, too," Joanie said.

"I noticed that, too," added Margie.

Of all the issues pressing down on Marie, one concern may have scared her most. She had morning sickness, stirring fears of another pregnancy ending with still birth. Butch could no longer overlook her visible struggles. He summoned Dr. Robert Smith, who made previous house call visits. After examining Marie privately in the couple's bedroom, Dr. Smith stepped out and asked Butch to join them in the bedroom.

"Mr. Beecher, I must tell you what I've just told your wife. First, it appears that she is pregnant. Second, I believe there is a problem with her central nervous system. We need to understand what is happening as soon as possible. Mr. Beecher, we need to get your wife to the hospital. I would be happy to help make the arrangements for you."

"If they're going to put me in that stupid box again, I'm not going. I get claustrophobic. I won't do it anymore," Marie declared, anticipating a return to the psychiatric ward for more hydrotherapy. "I can't be away from the girls anymore."

"That's not what I am talking about, Mrs. Beecher," Dr. Smith clarified. "I want you in the general hospital for a thorough examination. I want to have some blood tests done and some other testing done, as well."

"Pregnant? Are you sure?" Butch asked.

"*I'm* sure," said Marie, not waiting for the doctor to speak. "I haven't had my menses. I feel all the things I've felt before. I know what I know."

"All the more reason why we need to understand what's happening, for Mrs. Beecher and the baby."

17.

AT LAST

"Good morning, Mrs. Beecher," greeted Dr. Mitchell, Marie's attending hospital physician. "I don't have all your test results yet, but there is enough evidence that I can tell you with certainty, you are suffering from paresis."

"I'm not sure what you mean by paresis," Marie stated.

"It's late stage syphilis, ma'am. Did you know you have syphilis?"

Marie looked at him in shock, unable to muster a verbal response.

"I'm sorry to be telling you this, but you've had syphilis for quite some time. Are you sure you weren't aware of this?"

"Of course, I'm sure."

"Does your husband know? Have you had intercourse with anyone other than him?"

"No! No. No. No! No to everything! What kind of person do you think I am?"

"I'm sorry, Mrs. Beecher. I don't mean to imply anything. I know these are very personal questions, but we need to know what your history of sexual contact is, for your sake and the sake of anyone else who may be affected."

"My husband is the only one. There's never been anyone else."

"Will your husband be visiting today? There are more details and questions that I need to talk through with both of you."

Marie would not respond any further. Sensing she needed time to herself, Dr. Mitchell agreed to return later and left her room. He called to discuss her diagnosis with Dr. Smith, who agreed to contact Butch. Minutes later, the phone rang at the Beecher residence. Marie's father answered. John was there, taking his turn with getting his granddaughters off to school and watch over Joanie. He summoned Butch, who was outside in the garage.

"Butch – the doc's on the phone. He wants to talk with you."

Butch followed John back in and picked up the phone.

"Mr. Beecher, this is Dr. Smith. I received a call from the hospital. They have a diagnosis. It would be best that you go there to discuss your wife's condition. I also need to ask you some . . ."

"Just tell me the diagnosis, goddammit!"

"It's neurosyphilis, sir. It's an advanced stage of syphilis that is affecting her central nervous system."

Butch had no words.

"Mr. Beecher? Are you still there?"

"Yes."

"I strongly suggest you get to the hospital at your first opportunity. Ask to speak with Dr. Mitchell. I believe he'll be there today until 6:00 this evening. He'll go over things with both you and your wife. It's important that we determine whether you or your children may also be affected."

Butch agreed to be there within an hour and hung up the phone. John was sitting nearby at the kitchen table. He anticipated an explanation. Butch stood frozen in thought, as if John wasn't there.

"Well, what's the word?" John asked.

His son-in-law paused for several seconds. His mind was spinning to absorb an array of heart-pounding thoughts: *If he's right, I did it . . . I gave it to her . . . I must have syphilis.* He collected himself just enough to utter a safe response.

"He said she has some sort of nervous system problem."

"Well, what is it? What does that mean?"

"I don't know. I have to go in so he can explain it all to me and Marie."

Butch left behind his perplexed father-in-law and drove off to the hospital. A swirl of denial and deflection likely swirled in his head: *Maybe Marie got it on her own, maybe she was having extramarital sex of her own; maybe she contracted it some other way; is that even possible? how do I explain this? What do I do? What do I say?*

He asked for Dr. Mitchell at the reception desk and waited for him to appear, as if the doctor's presence would buffer the confrontation of truth he was about to face. Five minutes later, Dr. Mitchell greeted Butch. They rode an elevator to the fourth floor and entered Marie's room. The couple's eyes met. Butch froze initially and then stepped over to kiss Marie. She stared at him, her body language ice cold, refusing to acknowledge the kiss her husband placed on her cheek. Dr. Mitchell launched into a review of his findings, while making clear that Marie's illness was a sexually transmitted disease.

"These are uncomfortable questions, but they have to be asked," he began. "Have either of you had extramarital sex during your marriage?"

A deafening pause hovered for several seconds. Marie turned her eyes toward her husband with piercing condemnation.

Butch could barely maintain eye contact with either of them, trapped under the spotlight of inescapable guilt.

"You know it's YOU. Tell him. Tell *us*!"

Seconds ticked. Finally, he broke his silence.

"Years ago. A long time ago. Before I was a cop."

"Oh, baloney sausage!" Marie shot back. "I don't believe that for a second. You had your women back then, and who knows what you've been up to, hiding behind your goddamn uniform."

"How long ago, sir? How far back can you say?" Dr. Mitchell probed.

"Ten years. Maybe more," Butch admitted.

"In most cases, it takes at least ten years for the neurosyphilis infection to impair spinal cord and brain function," Dr. Mitchell stated. "That would account for the prolonged and progressive symptoms of the disease that you have experienced in recent years, Mrs. Beecher."

Butch stared at the wall. Marie stared at him, tears trickling down. Heartbreak personified.

Doctor Mitchell directed his words solely to Butch. "I'll do what I can to help your wife, Mr. Beecher. But I also need to run blood tests on you and your children, too. It's a simple process. We draw a blood sample. Then we perform what's called a Hinton flocculation test. It's the most accurate method available to identify the presence of the syphilis virus."

Butch nodded.

"It's imperative that we determine who is affected," continued Dr. Mitchell. "Based on all of the family history your wife has shared with me, I am particularly concerned about the health of your third daughter. I will also say that it is probable that the stillbirth of your son was caused by the presence of syphilis during your wife's pregnancy."

"What about my baby?" Marie asked, certain she was with child and terrified over the possibility of another dead child.

"Quite honestly, what I am about to tell you is a double-edged sword. The good news is, if you are pregnant, and, I think you are, women with late stage syphilis are no longer contagious. Prospects are still good for a healthy baby. What I'm about to tell you is harsh. The bad news is, and I am so sorry to say, your condition is advanced. There is no cure. In time, patients usually become incapacitated physically and mentally. The complications can be fatal."

Marie covered her mouth with her left hand. When he finished speaking, Marie covered her mouth with both hands for several seconds. She turned her face away from them and sobbed.

"Mr. Beecher, we can draw your blood sample today, while you are here."

The two men stepped into the hallway. Dr. Mitchell summarized treatment steps for Marie.

"With a positive response to treatment, it's possible she could be released in a week, maybe two. We want to be sure she's not a danger to herself. We'll do our best to prepare her to cope with her symptoms during pregnancy. It can be done. I've seen it before."

All Butch could do was nod, his thoughts still processing the array of emotions confronting him – shock, denial, shame, anger, fear.

"We can get your testing started right now. A simple blood draw. It won't take long."

"Okay."

"Now, based on what your wife has shared regarding your third daughter's health, I am concerned that she may be luetic. I would like you to bring her in as soon as you can, so I can examine her and draw a blood sample."

"What does that mean, luetic?"

"The health issues your daughter has may have syphilitic origins, especially when we know the mother has had syphilis for quite some time. Your girl may have contracted syphilis during pregnancy or birth. See one of my nurses at the station down the hall on the left before you leave. I'll go let them know you'll be coming down after you finish visiting your wife."

Dr. Mitchell shook Butch's hand and walked away. Butch stood for moment, then sat on a nearby bench. As he pulled out his pack of Kool's, he noticed the sign right in front of him – NO SMOKING. He had no choice, he had to go back in and face his wife, cold turkey. He reentered and sat on a chair next to Marie's bed.

"We'll get through this, Marie. I promise."

She eventually looked his way, closed her eyes and slowly shook her head.

"Not a word about this to the children. To anyone. Not one word."

"The doctor wants to see Joanie and do some tests. How do I explain that?"

She thought for a moment. "Just say you're bringing her here because I'm worried about her and want to see her. Just tell her sisters only one child can visit at a time. They'll understand."

Time passed. They sat in silence.

Butch rose. "I have to go to the nurse's station to talk about bringing Joanie in."

She spurned his attempt to kiss her. He headed down the hall to get his blood drawn and drove home.

The next day, Butch was back with five-year-old Joanie. Hospital staff allowed her to visit her mother briefly. Then, Joanie spent the next three hours with Dr. Mitchell and his staff. When little Joan came through two swinging doors to approach her father in the waiting area, she was licking a sucker with one hand and holding a nurse's hand with the other.

"This is my friend, Nurse Sally," Joanie told her daddy.

"Mr. Beecher, we're all done. You have a brave and sweet little girl. Dr. Mitchell will be contacting you in a few days. Thank you."

"Goodbye, Joanie. Maybe I'll see you again," said the nurse as she leaned down with a parting smile. Joanie nodded and smiled while savoring her sucker, then turned and looked up at her father.

"Can we see Mommy again?"

"No. I don't have time. Let's go."

He held his right hand out, and Joan raised her tiny left hand to his. A father with a lot on his mind, walking slowly to allow his daughter to finish her Tootsie Roll Pop.

"You'll have to finish that. No eating candy in the car."

When they reached the car, Butch tossed her candy stick as he opened the driver's door. He lifted her onto the seat. Joanie scooted over to where her mother normally sat. Her father began their drive home.

"I don't want you to talk about the things you did with Nurse Sally."

Joanie looked at him quizzically.

"It's okay to talk to your sisters and Grandpa John about seeing your mother, but I don't want you to talk about the things you did with Nurse Sally and Dr. Mitchell. That's our secret. Just between you and me. You understand?"

Joanie agreed with a reluctant nod.

They returned home, where life went on without the lady of the house. By now, Carol and Margie had grown accustomed to their roles as elementary school girls, housekeepers and sister-mothers to Joanie. Butch danced around questions asked by his in-laws, saying the doctors are trying to figure out how to treat Marie's neurological problems. He tried visiting Marie twice. Both times, she would only ask if there was word yet on their daughter's test results. She had nothing else to say.

Marie's treatments were an ordeal. A nurse told her she was about to receive electropyrexia treatment, an artificially induced fever therapy. It would involve confinement in a prone position for six hours in a steel hyperthermia cabinet, administered every other day.

"I am not doing that. I told my husband to make sure I would not have to go through that anymore."

"I'm sorry, Mrs. Beecher, we have to follow Dr. Mitchell's treatment plan. I promise to make this as comfortable for you as possible."

"And what if I refuse?"

"Please. I don't want to bring in an orderly to force you. Please trust us. Dr. Mitchell is the best man in town to treat what you have. Please, trust what we are doing to help you and your baby."

Marie finally relented. Disease controlled her fate. The men in her life controlled how to deal with it.

———————

Eight days after Joan's testing, Dr. Mitchell contacted Butch to review their test results with both husband and wife present. Butch took time off work the next morning and drove to the hospital, where the three met in Marie's room.

"Mr. Beecher, you tested positive for syphilis. Your disease is in what is termed as, late latent stage, which means you are asymptomatic and noninfectious. You may be fine going forward, but there is the chance you could develop tertiary syphilis symptoms like your wife. We can't predict if or when it will happen. It could be many years from now, perhaps decades later."

"Okay," Butch acknowledged quietly. He remained stone-faced, as both he and Marie waited to hear about Joan's condition.

"The various tests I performed on your daughter confirmed what I suspected. She has congenital syphilis. It's why she has dental deformities and an abridged maxillae, or upper jaw bone formation. It accounts for her lethargy, underdeveloped growth, anemia and skin abnormalities." He looked at Marie and continued. "The chronic colds, runny nose and laryngitis bouts you've told me about are caused by syphilitic rhinitis, commonly known as snuffles. Regarding her generalized nervousness and anxiety, as you can understand, it is typical of what diseased children go through. She has some brain function impairment, although I would characterize it as milder than the average child her age, which is an encouraging sign. Overall, her physical manifestations are also less severe than what we sometimes see. The affects are not reversible, nor are they curable. Going forward, she may very well survive but you can anticipate her health struggles will be an ongoing challenge. Her cognitive abilities are stunted. She will always struggle with learning and day-to-day activities."

Marie appeared perturbed. "Dr. Smith examined Joanie a few times during house calls. Why didn't he diagnose her earlier?"

"Symptoms of syphilis mimic so many illnesses. It can be very difficult to pinpoint it until the proper testing is done, as we've now done. When I examined her, she seems to be maintaining right now as well as can be expected."

Marie had heard enough. At last, she understood why her ailments went well beyond the heartbreak of losing a child. At last, she knew why Joanie was frail and plagued by sickness.

18.

TWIST OF FATE

F ather Devlin saw Marie several times during her hospitalization. Placing trust in his oath of confidentiality, Marie divulged the full extent of her reason for being there. He encouraged her to hand her fate over to God. She returned home in May.

Whether it was her confessor's inspiration or pure survival instinct, Marie returned home in May with a powerful message for the girls right from the start.

"My darlings, God has given me a chance to have a baby again. I have faith things will go better for us this time. I still might need your help sometimes, but, if we all have faith, everything will be fine."

As time passed, the girls were surprised by their mother's newfound assertiveness with their father: *Take the girls to the park . . . read the comics to Joanie . . . take Margie swimming . . . go practice baseball with Carol.* Seeing their dad happily comply was just as surprising.

"Isn't it weird how Mama tells Dad what to do now?" Carol asked Margie. "And he doesn't say no or anything. He just does it."

Margie agreed. "I know. It's like since Mama came home from the hospital this time, Dad's been extra nice, like he really feels sorry for her."

"I like that Dad works during the day," Carol remarked. "I hope things stay like this from now on."

It may have been the best summer they ever had together. Carol discovered she'd inherited her father's baseball talent. It brought her new-found acceptance and confidence. Now, instead of the boys picking on her for her extra weight, they fought over whose team she would play on.

"Ma, Ma!" Carol shouted as she burst through the front door on a July afternoon. "I hit a home run to win the game! It was so funny. Billy Jacobs, the boy that always picks on me, was pitching when I hit the home run. The boys were teasing *him* all the way home."

"Good for you!" her mother replied. "That'll teach that bully a lesson. I'm so proud of you, sweetie!"

Carol also took after father when it came to swimming. They were both *Chickens of the Sea*. Though Butch didn't swim, Margie took to swimming like a Wisconsin Muskellunge. He took her several times to the Washington Park pool four miles away. He'd drop her off, make a tavern stop and pick her up an hour later. Margie also went along with Aunt Dot and Uncle Jerry to swim in Pewaukee Lake, a half-hour's ride west on Capitol Drive. She frolicked in the water with her younger cousins Mary and Jerome Jr., capped off with Fudgsicles Aunt Dot would buy from an ice cream truck that cruised up and down the Wisconsin Avenue beachfront. The frozen, chocolatey treat was all the rage that summer, thanks to Fudgsicle ads on the popular *Popeye* radio show.

Joanie's bonding time with her father didn't measure up. He read her books and walked with her to a small neighborhood park, usually accompanied by one or both of his other daughters. Joanie's physical abilities were limited. Unfortunately, her father never quite knew how to deal with her.

The Beecher Sisters – Margie, Joanie, Carol. Circa 1938.
(A photo Cousin Julie found scrunched in her mother's
personal effects after her death in 2011.)

That summer, they moved into the house next door at 4126 North 26th Street.

It may have been Marie's most difficult pregnancy. Aside from the tremendous emotional strain of her paresis secret, nausea plagued her more so than ever before. In his house calls, Dr. Smith advised her to drink extra water to avoid dehydration, particularly during the warmer than usual summer. Her stomach had grown larger, and she gained more overall body weight compared to her past pregnancies. Marie insisted that the doctor never divulge her illness to anyone. Dr. Smith was keenly aware of the full extent of the courageous battle Marie was engaged in. She coped with her pregnancy as well as humanly possible under the circumstances.

On Saturday, October 29 she made her fifth trip to Mount Sinai's maternity ward, enveloped by both fear and dogged determination, as if she were a soldier facing a life or death situation. Two afternoons later, on Monday, October 31, Marie gave birth.

"It's a boy!" Dr. Smith called out.

At the sound of her son's cries, she melted with relief.

"Stay ready," Dr. Smith alerted. "There's another one."

"What?" Marie shrieked.

"Mrs. Beecher, there's another baby. Just hang in there and keep your breathing going," one of the nurses instructed.

"Oh my God! Oh my God!" Marie howled.

One half-hour later, Marie gave birth to another boy. To her great relief, the delivery room's head nurse confirmed that both boys appeared to be healthy and normal.

"I want to just say something. My husband is probably out there waiting. You can give him the news, but I want to be alone for the rest of the day. Tell him he can see me and the babies tomorrow. I want to be alone with my babies tonight. Please don't ask me why. I really mean it. Just respect my wishes, please."

The three nurses looked to the doctor for direction.

"Of course, Mrs. Beecher," Dr. Smith assured. We will inform him you gave birth to twin sons and that I've ordered complete rest and privacy for you until tomorrow. How is that?"

"Thank you, doctor. Thank you all. God bless you."

Marie was wheeled back to the maternity ward while one of the nurses headed to the waiting room and broke the news to Butch and Marie's father, John. Of course, they were shocked and amazed. The nurse assured the men that both babies were healthy and conveyed Dr. Smith's orders for rest and privacy until the next day. Father and grandfather dashed off to spread the word and celebrate.

In the morning, after the girls left for school, Butch drove to the hospital, dropping Joanie off at John's house en route. When his eyes met Marie's in the hospital, her forgiving spirit allowed her to enjoy the moment with him, despite the heartbreak he would forever embody to her.

"I know you were thinking of Carroll, Jr. if it was a boy. Now, we have to rethink things, don't we?" Marie quipped.

He could only nod with a slight smile. His mouth disarmed by so many things. A hangover. Lack of sleep. Dueling emotions swinging between joy and fear: *a son, two sons, two boys. Are they really healthy? Or do they have syphilis? Two mouths to feed, five kids. She's fucked up, my fault. How can she manage? Can she do this? Can I do this?*

Butch deferred to the moment. Overwhelmed by his plight, he never anticipated having to name two babies. It didn't matter to Marie. She had already decided.

"I like James and John. Those are the names I want."

"Two great names from the Bible," Butch acknowledged. "Sounds good to me. You did great, Ree. I'm so proud of you."

Non-identical twins Jim and John were baptized on December 12, the same day that Daniel had been stillborn four years earlier. It was a Monday. Sunday was the traditional day for the sacramental rite of new Catholics. Marie insisted on the 12th. Pastor Larsson at Saint Agnes Church understood Marie's symbolic intent and was more than happy to accommodate it.

The momentum of Marie's maternal drive carried her through the holidays. Mothering five children, including two infants, while privately facing the horrors of syphilis finally began taking a toll a few months later after the holiday season passed. Sheer will had powered Marie through a year of mental and physical torment that might have destroyed some women.

The *Great Pox* began to reestablish its gradual onslaught. Another shock wave of disruption and uncertainty was about to descend upon the Beecher family.

19.

OVER THE RAINBOW

Marge and Joan sat on the living room floor, transfixed by the illuminated dial of their RCA Victor radio console and the sound from its speaker.

"J-E-L-L-O!" A trio sang the radio show's opening theme, followed by the host's usual introduction. "The Jell-O Program, starring Jack Benny, with Mary Livingston, Phil Harris, Kenny Baker and yours truly, Don Wilson."

As was customary, the show opened with a song, and, on this Sunday night, a brassy rendition of "Sing, My Heart" blared from the radio. It was February 12, and a festive show unfolded to celebrate Jack Benny's birthday, as well as the upcoming Valentine's Day.

Marie sat in an upholstered chair, expressionless, with baby John cradled in her left arm while feeding him formula from a bottle in her right hand. Carol sat next to her mother using a chair from the kitchen, gently rocking baby James as he sucked a pacifier and waited to be fed by his mother. Whatever radio shows or movies Marie liked, her girls liked, too. Carol and Marge were accustomed to laughing along with their mother at the Jell-O Program. Younger Joan didn't always understand what was funny, but, if everyone else laughed, she laughed, too. Marie wasn't smiling or laughing during the show as she once had. Her blank look was the face of a heart without a song. Her girls would look at each other as they laughed. Sometimes, they turned to look at their mother, hoping to see her sharing in on the fun as she used to. Her body was there, but her smile, her light, was gone. The reassuring beauty of her soft, kindly voice was mostly silent, as if she hadn't the energy or interest to speak. "Carol" was the only word she uttered that evening, when she summoned her eldest daughter to help tend to the infants. Since the holiday season, her words came with the deliberate plainness of a woman under the spell of a Bela Lugosi trance.

Another unsettling trait had surfaced the day before, when Dorothy and Jerry stopped by for a short visit. Dorothy talked about it with Agnes in a Monday morning phone chat.

"Hi, Agnes. Did you listen to Jack Benny last night?"

"Oh, yes. God, did I laugh when Mary (Livingston) guessed his age and yelled *shut up*. Say, how was Marie when you stopped to see her Saturday?"

"Actually, that's really why I called you. It was the strangest thing. Marie called and asked me to pick up a few things from the store on the way over. We get there and I go into the kitchen, give her a peck, and I take out the evaporated milk she wanted. She started yelling at me: PET! You bought PET? Carnation, I wanted Carnation! Why would you do that?"

"Huh? Why would she say that? Why does it even matter?"

"Well, it shouldn't, but here's the really weird part. After she says that, she looks at Jerry and she yells, sort of half-crying: you *know* I wanted Carnation for Danny, how could you do this to me? How could you do this!?"

"Oh, my God. What's happening to her? What did Jerry say?"

"He didn't know what to say. He was shocked. We both were. I just stood there thinking, oh my God, she's delusional now. She looked very confused, and then it's like she came out of it and realize we were there. All she said was, 'Oh, I'm sorry, Dorothy. Thanks for the milk.'"

"Oh, God, that really scares me, Dorothy. Did Butch see that? Did the girls see it?"

"No. He was in the living room, joking around with the kids, doing those silly things that he does. It makes me wonder if he's sees what's happening or if he's just ignoring it. We're going there again tomorrow night after supper. I want to get a private moment with Butch."

Indeed, she did, recounting the details with Butch about Saturday's disturbing incident.

"She's a mess sometimes. It comes and goes. What do you expect me to do, put her in the psych ward again? I've got five kids to care for now."

"I know. I'm not saying that's what you should do. We're just very concerned, and I wanted to know if you've been seeing what we saw."

"I have. Look Dot, I appreciate all the things you do to help. Jerry, too. But unless she starts staying in bed all day again, she's better off here."

"Of course. Keep letting us know how we can pitch in. We'll do whatever you ask."

When John got word of his oldest daughter's latest malady, he called Butch with a proposal.

"I'm thinking of having a get-together here at 2:00 this Sunday afternoon after the last Mass at Gesu. I'd like you to be here. I heard Marie is relapsing again. I want us all to talk through how we can help, like we've done before, but while Marie is home."

"I don't know if that's really necessary, at least not yet."

"Just hear me out, okay? If Marie has help with the babies and things around the house, it might help her cope better, you know, take some pressure off. Who knows, it might stop her from backsliding. What I *do* know is, if she's away from her babies, it will kill her."

"Yeah, that all makes sense. I'll be there."

"Good. Agnes and Dorothy feel like they have to do something but, you know, they're afraid to overstep. I'm sure you can understand."

"Do you want to ask your sister to join us?"

"I'll call Minette. I'm sure she'll want in."

By the end of the *Summit of Leicht*, plans called for Dorothy and Agnes to take turns with 24-hour stints on weekends. Each stay would run from 7 p.m. to 7 p.m., one shift starting on Friday night, the other on Saturday night. Agnes could still work her stenographer job at Wisconsin Telephone Company without disruption. Dorothy's role worked, thanks to husband Jerry's willingness to spend part of each weekend caring for their own kids. Minette would make one visit each weekend, for an activity with the girls and help as needed. On weekdays, John would drive to the Beecher's two or three times weekly to observe and support, while keeping Marie company. It proved to be the best possible approach for all concerned. All were invested. All could see for themselves. Only one in her circle of support knew the full truth.

Agnes embraced her role, becoming closer to the Beecher girls than ever. A trip downtown in August became an emotional bonding experience for years to come. To help celebrate Margie's eleventh birthday on Sunday August 19, they went to see *The Wizard of Oz* movie, showing exclusively at the Wisconsin Theatre. Situated on Wisconsin Avenue just east of 6th Street, the Wisconsin's huge vertical neon sign dueled for attention with the glitzy marquee and similar vertical sign of the Palace Orpheum. In the 20th Century's midsection, the verve of Milwaukee's downtown never failed to quicken the pulse.

For three girls escaping a home encumbered by affliction, their seminal moment came when Judy Garland, in her role as Dorothy Gale, sang the film's heart rending, signature song – *Somewhere Over The Rainbow*. Like Dorothy, they too, yearned to leave troubles and worries behind. For a little while, the Beecher sisters flew to that place for twenty-five cents each.

1940. Hollywood was on a roll, producing a run of classic movies that were woven into the fabric of family memories. In late January, *Gone With the Wind* premiered in Milwaukee at the Palace Orpheum. It was shown exclusively at the Palace for five weeks, in a competitive retaliatory shot across the street at the Wisconsin for its exclusive run with the *Wizard* five months earlier. An afternoon matinee cost seventy-five cents, or one cent per every three minutes of the epic's two hundred thirty-eight-minute run time. Carol and Margie saw it for a second time on the last Saturday of February. Grandpa John gave them a ride home, where their aunt was preparing supper in the kitchen. Their mother and Joan played with the twins nearby.

"Well, did you like it as much the second time?" asked Aunt Dot.

"It's still the best movie ever!" Carol declared. "I could see it a hundred times."

"It was good. I liked it better the first time," was Margie's take. "It's just *soooo* long."

Having seen the movie herself, her aunt agreed. "I can't argue with that, though you really get your money's worth. And that Clark Gable. What a dreamboat!"

"Now, now, Aunt Dot," joked Carol. "You've got Uncle Jerry. You'll have to leave Rhett Butler for me."

Dorothy laughed and shifted attention to her sister. "Marie, why don't you go see it? It's only playing a few more days."

"What?" asked Marie. She wasn't following the conversation. Dorothy repeated the question. A haggard looking Marie shook her head and uttered, "No." Her will to speak would rise and fall occasionally between catatonic spells, as if she were dissolving in and out of a painting.

A few days later, Butch's old acquaintance Hattie McDaniel won a Motion Picture Academy Award for Best Supporting Actress in her role as *Mammy* in Carol's all-time favorite movie. McDaniel, whose parents were former slaves, became the first black American to win an Oscar.

As for Butch, his Bureau of Investigation stint ended. On March 2nd, he returned to his Patrolman role in District Five. His "award" was a bump up, from third shift to second. He had yet to attain enough seniority for a spot on first shift. His change in work hours altered the daily household rhythm again. At some point, the family sleeping arrangements also changed. Marie now had the master bedroom to herself, with the twins in the other first floor bedroom down the hallway. Upstairs, the three girls had one room, their father the other.

With their mother's unpredictable activity level, Carol's family role was now more parent than child. The same could also be said for Margie. In the first week of June, their summer school break began. Carol turned 14.

20.

THE WALK HOME

"I hate that smell," said Joanie. She stood on the grass of their small front yard, shading her eyes from the morning sun as she looked left toward the source of the oily stench.

"You won't have to smell it for long," assured Carol, as she and Margie placed their 20-month old brothers into the Radio Flyer wagon staged on the sidewalk next to Joanie.

Just after 9:00 a.m., the Beecher five began rolling right on the 26th Street sidewalk to escape the odor wafting from the roof tarring project atop Saint Agnes School. Their mother was still in bed. Their father had yet to return home from work. They headed north, crossing three streets and passing about twenty-five houses in the neighborhood of tightly packed properties. Their destination – Garden Homes Park, an oblong shaped green space, minute in size compared to the sprawling tracts that typified Milwaukee County's park system. The tiny park had the essential children's amusements – a huge sandbox, swing sets, slides, monkey bars and spinning contraptions. It offered a welcome escape for Carol and Margie, who had come to routinely stretch the caretaking time they would spend there with their younger siblings. Sometimes, they brought food in a picnic basket and a thermos of Kool-Aid to share.

Three hours passed. The twins were crabby and ready for

naptime. The five began to parade back home, crossing Atkinson Avenue onto 26th Street. Suddenly, the sound of a siren blared out ahead. Though still a good distance away, Carol and Margie could see a police squad car had turned from Capitol Drive onto their street. The sound of a second siren came forth. The squad car pulled to the curb on their side of the street. An ambulance trailing behind pulled to a stop directly behind the police car. After crossing Roosevelt Drive, the Radio Flyer quintet still had a block and a half to go.

"Are they at our house?" Carol wondered. She grabbed the wagon handle to help Margie pull a little faster. Their pace quickened. As they approached Hope Street, it became apparent.

"They're at our house!" Margie gasped.

Aside from the two emergency vehicles, the girls knew their father was home from the sight of his car in the driveway. Carol stumbled and fell. Their charge came to a momentary halt, yet as if in one continuous motion, she was back up and took off on her own.

"Carol! Wait! Carol!" Marge shouted.

Carol dashed across Hope Street, running down the sidewalk and across the patch of lawn in front of their house. She bolted up the porch steps and yanked the front screen door open.

Her rush through the foyer and into the living room came to an abrupt halt, instantly frozen by what her eyes beheld. Her fingers shot upward to cup her mouth, then quivered as she screamed in horror. Carol saw her mother's lifeless body lying on the floor in the kitchen, a pool of blood around her head. Four men looked at Carol as they stood near the body, startled by her sudden appearance – two ambulance attendants, an on-duty policeman and her father. The attendants rushed toward her with arms extended outward to block Carol's view. None of the men in the kitchen thought to stand watch by the door to prevent anyone, especially the Beecher children from entering. Butch joined the ambulance attendants as they grabbed Carol. Her legs buckled as they carried her back through the front doorway and onto the porch. She crumbled to her knees, crying out, "No, no, no, no!"

Out on the sidewalk, Margie pulled the wagon that carried the twins into the walkway leading to the porch, her face gnarled in fear by the scene before her. "Carol!" she screamed, as she threw herself up the steps and clutched her older sister by the shoulders.

"She's dead! She's dead!" Carol cried out.

Margie stared at her in horrified disbelief. Joanie stood in shock next to the wagon where her brothers sat in panicked fright.

"Mom's dead. I saw her, she's dead on the floor," Carol wailed.

Joanie began screaming. Their father knelt to comfort his two eldest daughters. His sons began crying in the wagon.

"Grab the boys for me, take them inside," he yelled to the ambulance attendants. "C'mon girls, upstairs now, let's go."

"We're coming in with the kids. You got her covered up?" one of the attendants called out to the policeman in the kitchen.

"Give me a second," the officer yelled back.

"Just go straight up," Butch ordered the attendants, pointing to the staircase leading up from the foyer. He helped Carol and Margie to their feet and stepped down to pick up his screaming youngest daughter.

The police officer left the kitchen, joining Butch to aid his stricken daughters with their ascent.

"Take care of your sisters and brothers 'til I come back up," he instructed Carol. "Put the boys there," he ordered the attendants, pointing to Carol's bed. "Let's go." The three men went down to return to the kitchen.

On their bed of pain, the five Beecher children spent the next few minutes in shared anguish. The sound of activity downstairs increased.

"I'll be right back," Carol said to Margie.

She walked into the hallway and down the stairs, where she saw her mother's covered body being wheeled out the front door on a portable gurney.

"Carol, get back upstairs," her father shouted. "I told you, stay up there 'til I come back up!"

She retreated, but instead of rejoining her siblings in the back bedroom, she entered the front bedroom to look out the window. Twenty to thirty onlookers had gathered in the street and on the sidewalk on the opposite side, staring as her mother's body was lifted into the back of the ambulance. In a surge of rage, Carol charged down the stairs and out the front door toward the street, beyond her father's reach.

"What are you looking at?" she yelled at the gawkers. "Mind your own damn business! Get the hell out of here!"

Butch rushed to her side and took her in his arms. She kept shouting while in his grasp.

"Go home, you creeps. You nosy ghouls!"

Butch forced her to turn around. The two reentered the house and returned upstairs. Outside, some of the neighbors *did* retreat, shamed by Carol's fire breathing admonishment.

"Your mother killed herself. She was so sad for so long, I guess she couldn't stand it anymore. She took my gun and shot herself. It's a terrible thing. She shouldn't have done it. We did everything we could to help her."

With Carol holding one brother and Margie the other, his five children wept in a cluster of grief.

"The policeman that was here is going to tell your Grandpa John. Your grandfather and your aunts will help us again, like they always have. Everything's going to be alright."

****

It happened Wednesday, June 26, 1940.

In 2016, I obtained a copy of my grandfather's Information Record from the Milwaukee Police Department. The single-page document contained three sections – 1) *Details and Promotions*, 2) *Meritorious Mention*, and 3) *Demerits*. Typed, one-line descriptions appeared in two of the three sections. Nothing appeared in the document regarding that day or the use of Officer Beecher's gun by a citizen/family member in a suicide death. While at the MPD Administrative Offices on Lisbon Avenue, I asked if a police report from 1940 might still be on file, specifically any record of a call response or death investigation that day at the Beecher residence. I was told it was extremely unlikely that such records still existed, especially for events prior to 1950.

21.

AFTERMATH

Father Larsson came to the Beecher house the next morning at Butch's request. The two men talked privately in the main bedroom on the first floor. Afterward, Butch came out and had Carol go in for her own private talk with their church pastor.

"Carol, your father asked me to speak with you. First, let me say, I am deeply sorry for your loss."

"Thank you," Carol quietly replied.

"Your poor mother struggled for years with the pain of little Daniel's death. She didn't mean to leave you and your sisters and brothers. It's just that her pain was so overwhelming, she couldn't take it anymore. She really died from a broken heart. You must understand that. It was a grave sin for her to take her own life, but God forgives her for it. He wants you to forgive her, too. Can you do that, my dear girl?"

Carol broke down as he spoke. She replied by nodding, her head hanging down, tears running down her cheeks. The priest offered his handkerchief. Carol dabbed her eyes as he waited for her to collect herself.

"I am reminded of the Lord's message in First Corinthians. My dear one, you must always remember, *GOD WON'T GIVE YOU ANY MORE THAN YOU CAN HANDLE.* You must do what the

Lord asks of you now. You are the eldest daughter. You must be strong. You must be strong for your father and for your brothers and sisters. Can you do that for Him?"

As she continued to dry her eyes and after several seconds, Carol nodded and replied, "Yes, Father."

"It's hard to believe right now, but you are going to be fine. I know it. You are a strong young lady. It's time for you to go out there now and make your father proud. Okay?"

Expectations were now conferred upon Carol in the heaviest of ways by God's representative. He approached Butch, who puffed a cigarette on the front porch while awaiting the priest's exit.

"Mr. Beecher, your daughter appears to be a brave young lady. She seems strong enough to do what has to be done. I think she is going to be fine."

"Thank you," Butch said, nodding politely while still appearing deep in thought as he gazed elsewhere.

"Before I leave, there is another serious issue I must inform you of. It's regarding the matter of conducting a funeral Mass. As you may know, the *Code of Canon Law* in the Roman Catholic Church dictates that those committing suicide must be deprived of ecclesiastical funerals. I'm sorry but Canon Law dictates that I cannot conduct a funeral Mass at Saint Agnes."

Butch turned his head; the sudden strength of his piercing eyes shattered all pretense of cordiality.

"Look, you've done a lot for me and I'm thankful. I really am. But you're *going* to do a service for Marie in your church."

"I'm sorry, but the matter is out of my hands. Archbishop Kiley would not approve of it," explained the priest, referring to the city's new archbishop, who had been newly installed just three months earlier.

"Bullshit! Archbishop Stritch was a family friend before he left for Chicago. If Kiley won't approve it, get in touch with Stritch.

Tell him it's for John Leicht's daughter. Believe me, he'll make an exception."

"I couldn't possibly do that. My duty is to the current archbishop. He's very much a traditionalist. I'm sure he would not allow it, nor would he appreciate my going over his head."

"Look, you Swedish meatball! I don't give a damn if the new guy has a stick up his ass all the way to Dublin. For Christ's sake! After everything Marie did with the Christian Mother's Society at your goddamn church?"

Clearly intimidated, the priest had no response.

"Hey," Butch continued with an accusatory finger point, "I know some things about you. I can cause some problems for you. Don't make me do that, alright? As far as you're concerned, it was an accidental death. That's it. You got it?"

With Butch's words and physical presence bearing down on him, the priest relented. "Alright. My apologies. I will start making all the arrangements. I'll make it work. Do you have a day in mind for the funeral?"

"The sooner, the better. I want my kids to get past all of this as soon as possible."

The Christian Mothers of Saint Agnes parish held a prayer vigil at O'Boyle Funeral Home on West Wisconsin Avenue, a mere city block from Church of the Gesu, where Marie had married Butch 15 years earlier. On Saturday, June 29, Father Larsson led the funeral Mass and presided over burial rites on the Clancy-Beecher family plot in Calvary Cemetery.

John drove with Agnes to the Beecher house the next day. He accompanied Butch and his three granddaughters to Sunday Mass at Saint Agnes Church. Agnes remained at the house to care for the twins. When Butch returned, Agnes implored him to accept her support.

"I have to be here for the children. I owe it to Marie to help them get through this."

"Agnes, I can't expect you to do any more than you already have. You have your own life to live."

"Butch, you don't understand. This *is* my life. Nothing else is more important to me right now. Dorothy has children of her own to care for. I don't. I *have* to do this for Marie. Let me stay here with the children, at least for a few weeks. You can't put this all on Carol so quickly. Put yourself in her shoes. My God, she needs time to grieve."

He accepted her offer, and, as the first days of July passed, the children's spirits were buoyed by the lightness of their aunt Agnes. Even Butch could see the calming effect of her presence, with an aura that mirrored Marie at her best.

"Are you going to stay with us from now on?" Joan asked.

"No, sweetie, but I will be here until your mommy in heaven tells me you will be alright without her."

Butch extended his leave from patrol duty through the second week of July. He also vacated his spot on the MPD baseball team, this time, for good. Over dinner on Tuesday, he proposed another change.

"I have to go back to work next week," he told Agnes and the children, before directing his attention to Carol. "I got offered a different job at work. I'm going to take it. I'll be a patrol wagon driver. It's a better job, but on the late-night shift that starts at midnight. Are you going to be okay with me being gone during the night?"

"I guess so," Carol's replied unconvincingly.

"Let's give it a try and see how it goes the rest of the month. Is that alright with you, Agnes?"

"Well, it's not up to me to say. I mean, it's your decision, Butch. Are you saying I should pretend to not be here at night or should I not stay the night altogether?"

"Stay, at least until the end of the month. While Carol gets used to me not being here."

At 12:00 a.m. on Tuesday July 16, Butch spent his first night away on the graveyard shift and as he preferred, free from possible queries from former shift mates about his wife's death.

Agnes continued to nurture her nieces and nephews for two more weeks. With the deadline approaching for registration at Rufus King High School, Carol received the talk she suspected was coming.

"Look, kiddo, I'm going to level with you. You know your aunt can't stay with us forever. With your mother gone, you're the lady of the house now. I need you home to take care of your brothers while your sisters are at school. It's what you have to do when you're the oldest. That's just how it is."

Marge turned twelve on August 18. Three weeks later, she started seventh grade classes at Saint Agnes School. Joan started first grade, one year later than usual for a girl her age. Knowing that she struggled with learning, her parents had hoped her delayed start with schooling might give her a better chance to succeed.

BEECHER. June 26 Marie Leicht Beecher, residence 41?'h N 26th st , wife of Carroll, mother of Carol, Margaret, Joan, James and John, daughter of Mr and Mrs John Leicht, sister of Mrs Jerome C Weirich and Mrs Louis Wilson and John Leicht. Funeral from the Funeral Home of J N. C Boyle Co 1214 W Wisconsin av., Saturday June 29 at 9 30 a m to St Agnes church. Interment Calvary. Members of Christian Mothers of St. Agnes' church will meet at funeral home Friday evening at 8 o'clock.

(Milwaukee Journal Death Notice – June 28, 1940)

Pictures of the Beecher children after their mother's death – Summer 1940
Left – Jim, Margie, John, Joan.
Right – Margie, their cousin Mary, my mother Carol.
(Photos by Jerome Weirich Sr. – September 6, 1937)

22.

SEEING RED

When his shift ended on Labor Day morning, Butch treated himself with a stop at *Sunflower Inn*.

"Hey Butch, good to see you!" Helen called out. "First one's on me, my boy. What's your pleasure?"

"Old Fitz."

Wap went the glass onto the bar. *Glug, glug, glug* went bourbon into the glass. "Here you go, kid. Breakfast of champions."

He raised his glass and gave Helen a nod. "Danke schön. Prost!"

"Haven't seen you in a while, Butch. Word gets around. Sorry to hear about your wife."

"Thank you, Helen. Life. Enjoy it while you can."

"Live a little! That's what I always say."

Helen went about her business, tending to holiday patrons craving a one-hundred proof morning. She kept a watchful eye on Butch. No sooner had he put down his emptied glass, Helen and Old Fitz were on him in an instant.

"I'm busy, so I can't gab with you as much as I'd like. Just wanted to tell you, a dame's been in here looking for you. Name of Ruth."

Butch shook his head. "I don't know of any Ruth."

"Whoever the hell she is, she sure seems to know you. Even left me her name and phone number." Helen turned to shuffle through a drawer behind her, then handed a slip to Butch. It read:

RUTH PLANT – BROADWAY 6669

He tucked the note in his left breast pocket while Helen waited for him to spill the beans about his mystery woman. "Thanks, Helen. When's the last time you saw her?"

"Mmmm, I'll say two weeks ago. She's a looker. Redhead, no less. If she's anything like me, you're gonna have your hands full. A spicy red tomato might be just the ticket for a pistol packin' son-of-a-bitch like you." The only woman in the world who could make him smile and blush pulled it off again. She moved on to serve other patrons.

As Butch lingered over his drink, it came to him. A woman named Ruth was a fan of the police baseball team. He remembered talking to a red-headed Ruth months earlier in the tavern where the boys hung out after a game. He moved the slip from his coat pocket to his wallet. Helen was too busy to talk. He left a dollar on the bar, gave her a wave and headed for the door.

"See ya', Butchie. You got a name and a number now. Go live a little!"

Five days later, curiosity won. He called the number on the slip.

"Hello?"

"Is this Ruth?"

"I'm her mother, Ann. Who's this?"

"Butch. She's been trying to get a hold of me. Can you give her a message for me? Tell her I'll be at the *Sunflower Inn* tomorrow 1:00 o'clock."

The next day, he got to the *Sunflower* at 12:45 p.m. and nursed his free one from Helen. Half an hour passed. Just when it seemed he'd been stood up, in walked Ruth.

"Well, hello there, Carroll. I'm so glad you called me. Sorry, I'm a little late. I'm usually running late, but I'm worth the wait." Right off the proverbial bat, her first pitch knocked him off balance.

"You did your homework, didn't you?" he said, a nod to her knowing his formal name. "My real friends call me Butch."

"Of course, Butch. Happy to oblige. When you left the baseball team, I heard your wife died. I'm so sorry for your loss. You know, I lost my husband five years ago. I divorced him. He's as good as dead to me. In a way, we have something in common. Someone we once loved died. I enjoy astrology. My cards kept telling me we had to meet."

"You get right to the point and then some, don't you?"

"I got *the treatment* the first time I came to this joint," she recalled. "I asked for a glass of red wine and all hell broke loose. Helen yelled out, 'Hey everybody, this one must've just got off the boat from France . . . wine?'"

"Why the hell would you ask for wine, in Milwaukee of all places?

"I lived in Montana for a while during Prohibition. I'd order wine bricks from Beringer's in California. They came with instructions – *dissolve the brick in a gallon jug of water but don't leave it in your cupboard for twenty-one days or it will turn into wine.* How about that? They actually told you how to make it into wine!" Ruth laughed. "Anyway, that's how I developed a taste for wine, and that's how I learned Helen only serves two kinds of the hard stuff."

They fed each other verbal choice cuts. Helen stepped over occasionally to garnish the repartee with spicy quips. Ruth discovered he had five children, he learned she had three – Delores, Bobby and Janice, ages 14, 13 and 8. There were commonalities.

Both of their oldest were girls the same age, both had mothers of Irish ancestry, both were raised Roman Catholic. Butch discovered another shared trait. Bodacious Ruth could keep up with him, drink for drink.

Butch checked his watch. "I've got to head home soon."

"I should, too. This isn't the best neighborhood to flag a cab. I wonder if I can use Helen's phone to call for one?"

"Don't bother, I'll give you a ride. Where to, ma'am?"

"839 North Cass Street."

"Two blocks down from St. John's Cathedral," declared Butch, flashing his street knowledge. "I'll have you there in 10 minutes."

When Butch pulled up to her apartment building, Ruth pointed down the street.

"Well, how about that? Here comes my kid, right now. I'll introduce you."

Butch left the car to join Ruth on the sidewalk.

"You must be coming back from the 'Y,' huh?" she said to her son. "Butch, this is my boy, Bobby. Bobby, this is Butch. He's a friend of mine and a heck of a baseball player."

Big bull Butch reached out and shook hands with the sinewy young buck.

"Nice to meet you, son. You play baseball, too?"

"No."

"Your mother tells me you do a lot of boxing at the YMCA. You must be good at it."

"Yeah."

"Three years ago, I saw Freddie Steele beat Gorilla Jones to win the middleweight title at the Auditorium. Have you ever seen a professional bout?"

"No. When I do, I'll be in it and knock the guy out."

"Like I told you," Ruth reiterated. "He's got a chip on his shoulder like that son-of-a-bitchin' old man of his." From their chat at the *Sunflower*, Butch knew that Bobby and his sisters lived most of their lives without a father around, just as he had.

****

She was a woman who knew what she wanted. He was a man who knew what he needed. Bing, bang, boom, eight months later they wed at the Milwaukee County Courthouse on May 23, 1941.

23.

DAY ONE

"Yesterday, December 7th, 1941, a day which will live in infamy."

F ollowing Japan's attack on Hawaii's Pearl Harbor, President Roosevelt used his historic radio address to forever brand a day in history. The United States officially entered World War II on December 8. In Butch and Ruth's world, their families had united in conflict seven months earlier, on June 8, the first day the *Beecher Ten* lived under the same roof.

———————

June 7, the second of two straight days of packing for the Beecher girls on 26th Street. Tommy Dorsey's current hit blared from the Philco radio in their living room:

> *Let's get away from it all*
> *Let's take a trip in a trailer*
> *No need to come back at all*
> *Let's take a powder to Boston for chowder*
> *Let's get away from it all*

Marge stood on a chair to reach some empty Mason jars stored on the top shelf of the pantry. They hadn't been touched since their mother placed them there. She passed the remaining jars down to Carol, whose eyes welled as she wrapped each jar in newspaper and place them in a cardboard box.

"Oh, God, I knew this would happen," Carol repined.

Marge stepped down from the chair with tears on her cheeks. Memories of the preserving skills their mother once possessed washed over them. "I know," she said, giving Carol a quick hug. "We have to try to not think about it."

It would be their last night of sleep in the house their mother had died in, 363 days earlier.

A moving crew pulled up to their house bright and early the next morning. Three wiry lads jumped out, each looked right out of high school. A car pulled into the driveway with Tommy Boy at the wheel. He and Butch had long since patched things up. One of Tommy's latest ventures was hauling services. His usual business model, of course – cheap labor, off the books, all cash, untaxed. His crew had already moved half of the family's belongings to Richards Street on Friday, the day they'd moved Ruth and her kids in. As noon approached, the caravan to a new life was set to go. In the back seat of their car, the eyes of three sisters fixed onto 4126 one last time. Not a word was spoken.

Twelve minutes later, they arrived at 2439 North Richards Street. It was an inviting house, two-stories with an attic under a gabled roof. A wooded porch spanned the front with vertical beams that supported a wood-fenced balcony above. Heartened by its sight, the Beecher siblings spent their next two hours on the second floor, unpacking things in the boy's room and the larger adjoining bedroom that their sisters would occupy. Across the hallway, the large bedroom claimed by their step siblings was all set up, though unoccupied.

When the Beecher's arrived, only Ruth greeted them at the door. Her brood was elsewhere, perhaps exploring the first non-apartment building neighborhood of their lives. Bobby appeared just as Tommy's crew had finished haul-in duties. Butch joined the crew street side, doling out handshakes and greenbacks. When the movers departed, Butch motored off with Bobby to do some final clean-up at 4126 . . . and Ruth's yap motored inside the house.

"Carol! Get down here."

Upstairs, the Beecher sisters froze and looked at each other. Never had they heard a woman beller like that, let alone inside the sanctuary of home.

"Carol Beecher! I know you can hear me up there! You heard me. I want you in the kitchen, this instant!"

Down went Carol. Her sisters followed, tip-toeing the steps of curiosity for a peak. While Carol unhooked the collapsible baby gate to enter the kitchen, her brothers stood on the other side, frightened by their bellowing stepmother.

"What took you so long?" asked Ruth, with no interest in hearing an answer. "Your father wants a nice first supper here," she continued, pointing to a few dinner recipe index cards laid out on the counter by Butch before he left. "I stocked up on food yesterday. You pick a meal and make it. Have it ready at 6:00."

"But I haven't finished unpacking. I'm helping Joanie get organized, too."

"Do your job here. You can do all that later. I need to lay down for a while."

"Why are you doing this? Delores is all settled in. Why don't you have her make supper?"

"I'll tell you why," Ruth said, moving face-to-face with Carol, accompanied by an alcohol/cigarette musk. "I hear you have lots of cooking experience. Delores doesn't. That's why!" In a sense, she was right. Her mother had done most of the cooking when Ruth and her kids lived at the Cass Street apartment. Ruth broke from her intimidation stance, turning to head to the bedroom. As she walked away, she fired off a parting shot, a finger wagging in the air. "Don't you ever question me, Missy. And don't make a lot of noise. I'm a light sleeper."

Carol broke down in tears. Marge and Joan rushed to her side. Joan began to cry for her. Marge held strong and offered a simple solution.

"We'll help you make supper. We'll do it together, just like we've done before."

Before long, Ruth's snoring reverberated from down the hall, giving the solidarity sisters reason to cackle. They closed ranks and turned fluster into fun, opting to prepare a favorite casserole dish their mother used to make.

"Shhhhh, be careful. Don't wake the witch," Marge whispered. Supper was readied with time to spare. Baking start time was five o'clock. On the cusp of 6:00 p.m., Ruth emerged refreshed, just as Butch entered with Bobby. Everyone gathered at the family dining table, now permanently expanded with the leaf previously reserved for holiday guests. Normalcy's pretense lasted five minutes. Then, Joan spilled the beans.

"She made Carol make supper so she could sleep," Joan said, pointing to Ruth. "Carol cried because it was unfair, but we helped her make supper. She's drunk. She's not nice like Mama was."

"What the hell is she talking about, Ruth?" Butch demanded, protective hackles instantly raised.

Ruth glared at Joan. "Your little one is blowing things way out of proportion."

Butch saw the truth in the faces of his five children. "I can see she's not blowing it out of proportion."

Ruth gestured with a "*phooey on you*" wave.

"All of you, keep eating," ordered Butch.

He got up and pulled his wife from her spot at the other end of the table. With a hand clamped into her armpit, he perp-walked her to their bedroom and slammed the door behind him. "First goddamn day and you pull this shit?" His words were clearly audible in the dining room, as were the slap and rumble sounds that followed. Gurgling accompanied his next words. "You pull this again, and I'll snap your neck, you goddamn bitch." Next came the sound of the bedroom door opening, followed by the sight of his steaming return to the table. Eyes ablaze. Breathing heavily.

"Finish what's on your plates. Go outside and play 'til it gets dark out."

Only the sounds of fork clangs on plates and the smack of casserole mastication followed. Butch had the dining room to himself in less than five minutes.

He went to the kitchen to pour himself a shot of brandy. After tossing it back, he went to the bedroom and opened the door. "Get out here and clean everything up."

Ruth was on their bed, reclined with her back against the headboard. She bore the smile of a *masochist* as smoke gently rose from the Lucky Strike between her fingers.

"You men. You're all alike. I should've known you'd be just like my first husband." She took another drag and exhaled seductively. "Do what you feel you have to do, Officer Beecher. But know this. I outlasted my first husband. I'll outlast you, too. "

He may have wondered: *Who did I marry, Cagney with head lights and a henna rinse?*

"Get this straight right now, Ruth. This is my house now. There's only one boss here. Me! You don't drink in my house unless I say you can."

"Sure, Officer Beecher, whatever you say," mocked Ruth. She tamped her cigarette in a nightstand ashtray, rose from the bed and walked past him with an eerily defiant grin.

Ruth cleaned up the dining room and washed all the dishes. At sunset, the children trickled inside and headed for their respective bedrooms. Each parent made sure their own children brushed their teeth. Each parent wished their own children goodnight.

Before succumbing to slumber, Marge asked Carol, "Don't you think it was weird that Bobby didn't seem to care what Dad did to his mother?"

"Maybe he thought she had it coming," Carol mused. "Maybe he wished he was the one giving her the business."

24.

WAR DIARIES

Uncertainty. Fear. Hate. Hope. Resolve. Mindsets of wartime. As 1942 unfolded, Milwaukee was transformed like the rest of America. No one knew what to expect or how long it would last. Men were leaving to join Allied forces in theaters of battle already being waged on several continents around the world. Milwaukee's *"Singing Mayor,"* young Carl Zeidler, resigned from his post in April to join the fight. The appearance of service flags in house and apartment windows signifying one or more family members fighting overseas became commonplace.

By year's end, shortages and rationing of goods were the norm. Sadly, dashing hometown hero, Carl Zeidler, was reported lost at sea off the coast of Africa. After hearing radio reports of the mayor's fate, Marge asked her Father, "Will you have to leave for the war, too?"

"Policemen are *Two A*. We get a deferment because we serve every day," explained her father. "The city still needs police. I'm not going anywhere," he added with a wink.

To the chagrin of his children, Butch now spent little time at home. Was it extra patrol duty keeping him away or tavern time?

A hard truth became increasingly evident to his children and Carol, in particular. It was Ruth's house to run. One issue was a hopeless battleground. Caring for little Jim and John would be an ongoing flashpoint of conflict between Carol and Ruth. In the days and weeks that followed their mother's tragic death, the Beecher children could not have imagined a future homelife with a woman so unlike their mother. A change of homes had thrust them from one crucible into another. Carol and Marge referred to it often in the diaries their mother taught them to keep. In the months and years that followed, the sisters chronicled their shared ordeal. Enduring the *Reign of Ruth*.

———————

Carol – July 2, 1941

I'm proud of myself for coming up with a nickname for her. The WICKED WITCH. She favors her own kids so much; they are like her flying monkeys. Delores is nice enough to me. But she knows her mother makes me do all the chores. She hardly ever makes Delores do any. She plays dumb like she doesn't notice. Bobby always fakes like he's going to punch me, but he never does. I like him, I guess. Margie really likes him. He can be pretty funny sometimes. Margie loves my nickname for her. She came up with a good one too. MISS GULCH.

Carol – August 30, 1941

God, I hate her. Today she said I'm too stupid to go back to school and that's why I want to stay home to take care of the twins. I tried telling her that I promised to raise the boys. She just makes fun of me and says I'm afraid to go to school. She always says mean things to me when no one else is around to hear her say it. I swear, she is evil. I'm glad that Dad is okay with me starting high school at Rufus King, so I don't have to go to Riverside with Delores. She thinks she's smarter than me just because she's a grade ahead of me. Her mother probably makes her think that way. Delores knows I had to take off from school when Mom died. As God as my witness, I'll show them, just like Scarlett O'Hara said.

Marge – November 1, 1941

The witch came home from her beauty shop work today and slapped me and Carol just because we made a birthday cake for the twins without her permission. Carol said we don't need her permission and she slapped her. So, I yelled at her and she slapped me too. Carol yelled at her and cried. I stood my ground and just stared at Miss Gulch. She slapped me again and I just stared at her and told her you can't make me cry. She laughed and slapped me again and walked away. I told dad about it when he got back home. He beat her up in the bedroom. I'm glad he did. I showed Gulch I'm not ever going to be afraid of her.

Carol – April 11, 1942

She took away the picture of Mom we keep in the bedroom just because me and Marge and Joan talked about it being Mom's birthday yesterday. She just came home from work and went up and took it off the wall and hid it. She said it's for our own good, so we stop thinking of Mom. Like taking her picture down is going to make us like her. Ha! She stinks like alcohol again. I can't believe they let her drink at the beauty shop. Maybe she goes somewhere to drink after. She is always extra angry after work on Saturdays. Unless Dad is home. Then she yells at him instead of me. He slaps her and tells her to shut up and then she smiles! I swear, she acted like she wanted him to slap her again. Dad yelled at Mom sometimes, but he never slapped her. Aunt Agnes couldn't believe it when she came over and found out the Wicked Witch took Mom's picture away. Aunt Agnes already hates her because she only allows her or Aunt Dot visit when she is gone working at the beauty shop. I told Aunt Agnes I call Ruth the Wicked Witch. She laughed and agreed with me. I really miss Mom these days

Marge – June 20, 1942

Dad took Joan to a doctor today. He didn't come home with her. He says she's going to be in a hospital for a while to help her think better. Poor Joan, I feel so sorry for her. I asked if we could visit but it's not allowed. I wish he'd put Ruth in a hospital to get her to not be such a hag.

Marge – September 16, 1942

Bobby is skipping out of class all the time now to go and practice boxing at the gym on Center Street. Gulch found out when someone from school called. She yelled at him, but she never slaps him like she does to me and Carol. She even slaps Joan sometimes. Bobby could take it because he's used to boxing but she never hits him. I think she is afraid he will beat her up. I don't think Bobby would ever do that. But he hates school. I really think he hates his mother as much as me. Delores and Janice are her pets. She never hits them. She never even yells at them. Only us. She is never going to stop hating us.

Carol – November 7, 1942

Toodles has been gone now for a week. Ruth said he ran off on Jim and John's birthday, when Dad took us to visit with Aunt Dot. Dad checked the Humane Society again today to see if the dog catcher found Toodles. I've been crying about it off and on all week. I swear, Ruth purposely let Toodles go. She knew he was mother's dog. I think Toodles reminded her of Mama. I wish I could prove she let it happen. God, I hate her.

Carol – June 6, 1943

Dad took us to Aunt Dot and Uncle Jerry's house. They had a surprise party for my 17th birthday. It was wonderful! Everyone was there, Grandpa and Aunt Agnes too. I felt so special. Of course, Witch Ruth refused to come even though she and her kids were invited.

BAD NEWS! The Weirich's are moving to California soon. Uncle Jerry got a job with the railroad there. I can't stand to think that they won't be here anymore. Aunt Dot reminds me so much of Mom and now she won't be around anymore either.

Marge – October 17, 1943

Miss Gulch was terrible to Joan today because she couldn't figure out her homework. Then she got mad at us because we kept trying to help Joan. She calls Joan a retard and stupid. She hurts Joan's feelings on purpose and tells her she will never be smart like Janice. Carol and I yelled at Gulch for being so damn mean. Joan has some things wrong with her, but she is not stupid. Gulch is giving us an extra hard time because dad is working all weekend. Even Bobby told her to stop doing it so much. She gets back at us by making food for her kids but not us. She told us to make your own supper. She went with Delores and Janice to see a movie. I'm glad they're gone. I wish they would never come back. I think Bobby does too. I wonder if he knows I like him.

Carol – December 25, 1943

The Wicked Witch's mother came to cook Christmas dinner. It was pretty good actually. Dad didn't have to work tonight. He was in a good mood all day. Even the Witch seemed happy all day. I bet she was just on her good behavior to show off how nice she is to her mother. She even told Delores to help clear off the dining table and wash dishes with me and Marge. What a phony baloney she is. She told her mother that Joan is such a sweet little girl and that her and Janice get along so well. God, I wanted so much to tell her mother that Ruth is a big fat liar.

Carol – May 5, 1944

It has been quite a time these last 2 days. Ruth coughed up blood during supper yesterday. Dad took her to County General today. She may be there for a few days. Dad told Marge and me today that Ruth had TB years ago and she has problems with her heart and lungs. I guess I should feel badly for her so I'm not calling her a Witch this time. Ruth's mother wanted her grandkids to come stay with her while Ruth is in the hospital. So, we have the house to ourselves! We walked down to Serio's and Dad treated us to a fish fry for supper. Dad goes there all the time when he is not on police duty. Everyone knows him there. It was the most fun we have had together in a long time. Marge and Joan are still laughing while I'm writing this. I'm really looking forward to not having Ruth around for a few days. I wish she'd never come back here.

Carol – May 12, 1944

What a difference a week makes. Dad brought Ruth back from the hospital today. Right away she went on and on that I have to do all the cooking and housework because she has to rest. Not Delores. Just me. She gave me a hard time about Dad taking us to Serio's last Friday. She said I bet you're glad I was in the hospital. It's like she could read my mind. I don't understand why she hates me so much. She thinks I'm in competition with her. All I have ever tried to do is get along with her. The Witch is back.

Marge – June 13, 1944

Dad put Joan in the hospital. He said it's the same place she went two years ago. Her one leg bothers her so much. Dad says they're going to help her with that and help her because she has fits sometimes. She gets so frustrated. I don't blame her. Poor Joan, she has so many problems.

Marge – July 2, 1944

Bobby made a big announcement today. He signed a contract to become a professional boxer. He always bragged about winning his bouts, but I did not think he was this good. Dad seems happy about it. Miss Gulch is furious because he is quitting school. He is going to California sometime next month to fight 2 paid boxing matches. I don't believe it. I am happy for him but I don't want him to get hurt. The thought of him not being here makes me sad. I don't dare tell him I am disappointed. I feel sorry for him because his own mother Gulch is not at all happy for him.

Carol – July 21, 1944
Dad quit the police force so he can work at Serio's. Dad and the Wicked Witch were fighting all day about it. The Witch was yelling at him and saying the police department made him quit because he's a drunk. He drinks but I don't think he is a drunk. He says he will be home more now so it will be good for the family. God, I hope so.

Marge – August 30, 1944
Bobby won his first match in San Jose, California. He called around midnight to tell Gulch. He knocked the other boxer out in the 3rd round. Everyone was so excited. Dad got up today and went down to Serio's. Bobby is the talk of the neighborhood. Dad said everyone at Serio's was talking about Bobby and the Szczepanski's across the street because there is a Gold Star Flag up in their window now. They have two sons in the war. No one knows yet which one got killed. Bobby has another match Friday night in San Francisco. I wonder if he will get to see the Golden Gate Bridge and the Pacific Ocean.

Marge – September 2, 1944
Bobby won again last night in San Francisco. This time he knocked the guy out in the 2nd round. He called this morning to tell his mother about it. Gulch still doesn't seem to be proud of him. He will take a train on Tuesday to come back home. I want to do that someday. A long train ride would be such an adventure. Maybe he will become famous. I hope he doesn't get hurt.

Carol – September 8, 1944

Bobby got back today. The Wicked Witch is forbidding him to continue boxing and told him he had to go back to school. Bobby got really mad. I was afraid he was going to punch her. I took the twins to the park to get them away from her like I always do when she's angry. I don't know if Dad will have anything to say about it. Bobby left the house very angry. I feel bad for him. I'm sure Marge feels worse. I know she has feelings for him but she doesn't like talking about it. I am wondering what will happen tomorrow. Dad is going back to work at the police department. He's probably sick of hearing the witch complain all the time.

Carol – January 1, 1945

Bobby left home today. He is moving in with another boxer that lives by the gym on Center Street. He's been working since he quit school, but he won't say where. The Witch said good riddance. How can she say that about her own child?

Marge – March 17, 1945

Gulch came home angry from the beauty shop yesterday right after Dad went to the bar. She took it out on Carol again. She picked on Carol the rest of the day, calling her names and saying she is stupid and lazy. I don't know how Carol puts up with it without losing her temper. Gulch must have said something Dad didn't like when he got home. He was yelling. She got a beating for Saint Patrick's Day. Good.

Carol – April 1, 1945

I found out Dad quit the police force again last week. He didn't tell me about it until today. He is going back to bartending at Serio's. We had a heart to heart talk. He just didn't want to do police work anymore. He just wants to be close to home to keep an eye on things. I think he feels bad because he knows Ruth has been such a terrible mother. I think he feels like it's his fault. He made a big mistake marrying Ruth and he knows it now.

Marge – April 10, 1945

It was an awful day. The Witch got hers though. As soon as Dad left for Serio's, Gulch was putting us down for making a cake in honor of mama's birthday. She said our mother is in hell because she killed herself. Carol got so angry, she yelled back at her and pushed her. Gulch smashed her empty wine bottle and threatened Carol with it. Carol grabbed a broom and swung it, knocking the jagged wine glass from Ruth's hand. But Carol dropped the broom and Ruth grabbed it. Carol tried to get away but Gulch kept hitting her with the stick end. Joan and Janice were screaming. I ran to Serio's to tell dad. He ran home and dragged the Witch by the neck down the stairs. Ruth must have chased Carol up there. Then he dragged her into the kitchen and mopped the floor with her. I was afraid he might kill her.

Marge – August 15, 1945

Thank God the war is over. The Japs surrendered. I have never seen everyone so happy. Carol and I took a streetcar downtown. I never saw anything like it. When we got home Gulch was drunk. She said – I hope you sluts didn't spread your legs for all the sailors. We just laughed and ignored her. I can't wait to tell Dad what she said. She'll get hers.

****

Ten months later, Ruth got hers, alright. She got dead.

25.

RUTHLESS

Friday, June 10. Butch woke to find Ruth unresponsive with a weak pulse and barely breathing.

"Operator, I need an ambulance. My wife's unconscious. The address is 2439 Richards Street."

A rescue squad came. They could not get her to regain consciousness. Ruth was taken to County General Hospital, with Butch trailing in his car behind. In the early morning hours of June 11, she was pronounced dead of heart failure.

Butch returned home to deliver the news to Ruth's daughters. Janice fainted. Marge and Carol, who had turned 20 nine days earlier, revived Janice and did their best to comfort her.

"I'm going to drive to Cass Street to notify your grandmother," Butch told Delores.

"I want to come with you," said Delores through tears.

After they left, Carol agreed to stay with Janice while Marge walked to Center Street in hopes of informing Bobby. He was nowhere to be found. Butch returned home at midday. At Ann Lee's request, he picked up Janice and took her to Cass Street. Ann wanted her granddaughters to spend the night grieving with her.

Carol woke in the middle of the night. Unable to sleep, she stepped out to the balcony to sit. Minutes later, Marge joined her.

"I couldn't sleep," Carol told Marge. "I still can't believe it."

"I know what you mean. I couldn't either. Isn't it weird? It's June, the same month Mom died."

"You're telling me? They both died right after I had a birthday. I'll never have a birthday again without thinking about it."

"Are you thinking what I'm thinking?" Marge asked.

"What?"

"We got what we hoped for. She's gone. I mean, it's terrible it happened like this. I feel so badly for Delores and Janice. We know how it feels."

"I hated her, but I didn't wish her dead."

"I kind of did. It's okay to admit it. I'm just being honest."

"Well, it's not like it's our fault. She had TB. A bad heart."

"Of course, it's not our fault. I couldn't sleep. I kept thinking how they both died of a broken heart."

For the second time in six years, Butch made burial arrangements for a wife. He called to ask Ann if she wanted to participate.

She declined and got right to the point. "I have to be honest. I never believed the two of you would last. Every day, I expected a call from Ruth to say she was done with you and your damn kids. It's never easy being married to a policeman."

"We tried to make it work."

"She never loved you. You never loved her. Just a marriage of convenience, that's all it was. Wouldn't you agree?'

"Look, Ann, I don't know why you're getting into all this right now. I just called out of respect. We never talked about what she wanted for a funeral. I thought you might know."

"No, I don't. All I ask is you give her a decent burial. She might have wanted to be buried in Minnesota with family. If you can afford that, fine. Otherwise, just do what you think is right and let me know what the plan is."

"I will, Ann."

"One more thing, Butch. I'd like you to pick up Delores sometime today. Bring her to the house and help her bring some belongings back here. The girls won't be staying there anymore. I want them here with me."

Two days later, Ruth was buried in the Clancy-Beecher family plot next to Marie at Calvary Cemetery. Bobby got word of his mother's death. He joined his sisters and grandmother for a brief graveside service. The six Beechers were there, along with a handful Ruth's co-workers.

On Sunday, Tommy helped Butch move the Plant girls' remaining belongings from the house to Ann's apartment. The two families would never see each other again. When they returned to Richards Street, they walked to Serio's to drink. Joe, Butch's bartending cohort, set the boys up with a shot and a beer each. They tapped shot glasses and Tommy offered a toast.

"Happy to help you get all this over with, my friend. To better days."

"Thanks, pal. Prost."

"Damn," Tommy said. "Now that I think of it, a few people got sick from that wine I gave out last Christmas. I gave Ruth one of those cases. I sure hope she didn't get sick from that. Hate to think I killed her."

"Don't say that," replied Butch. "Don't ever joke about that, either."

BEECHER-Plant: Ruth Ann (nee Lee), of 2439 N Richards st. Tuesday, June 11, aged 39 years, beloved wife of Carroll A Beecher, mother of Dolores, Janice and Robert Plant. Carol, Margaret, Joan James and John Beecher, daughter of Ann Lee, sister of Irene Hawker of Glen Rock, Wyo. Fenton J Lee of Des Moines, Iowa. Funeral Friday, June 14, at 8 30 a m. from the Froemming-Beecher Funeral Home, corner E North av and N 1st st to St Gall's church. Interment Calvary. In state Thursday after 10 a m.

(Milwaukee Journal Death Notice – June 13, 1946)

26.

CROSSROADS

Zip-a-dee-doo-dah, zip-a-dee-ay
My, oh, my, what a wonderful day
Plenty of sunshine headin' my way
Zip-a-dee-doo-dah, zip-a-dee-ay!

John Leicht enjoyed a renewed closeness to his grandchildren following Ruth's death. On the day after Thanksgiving, he took all five to *Songs of the South*, the newly released Walt Disney musical featuring the hit song, *Zip-a-dee-doo-dah*. Sung by actor James Baskett in the role of Uncle Remus, the catchy tune evoked the virtue of a joyful spirit in the face of hardship.

"What a great Thanksgiving holiday it's been. I've so enjoyed my time with you today," he told his grandchildren on the drive home. "I am so proud of all of you, and I know your mother is, too." John reveled in seeing his Beecher grandchildren happier than he'd ever seen before.

Back on Richards Street, a restless Butch found himself increasingly uncomfortable. While tending bar that weekend, he quizzed Tommy as soon as he arrived.

"Have you been running your mouth about my life?"

"I have no idea what you're talking about."

"Some rummies came in here, asking if I'm the dead wives' guy. Twice this month. Where the hell are they getting that from?"

"Oh, so that's *my* fault? I don't know anyone around here. You know that. Christ, get a grip."

"Where do they hear shit like that, then?"

"C'mon, you had to know this would happen. People knew you and Ruth fought a lot. Hell, you bitched about her yourself, right here in the bar. And Ruth, she could have told every dame in the neighborhood about your first wife. You know? They talk, talk, talk."

"Well, God dammit, I don't like it. I even had a copper from District Five. Haven't seen him in years, guy comes in, he starts giving me the third degree, too."

"Third degree? How so?"

"You know. Asking me how I've been, about my wives and how they died. Not about baseball or weather or whatever the fuck. Why would he do that?"

"Beats me. Was he here in an official capacity?"

"No. It didn't look like it. He stopped in with his wife. Said he didn't know I worked here."

"So, what did you tell him?"

"As little as possible. It's nobody's goddamn business."

"So, that's three guys that brought up a touchy subject. Anyone else?"

"No, but I get this feeling from people sometimes. The feel. It's not the same anymore."

"Relax already, will you? You're spooked. That's not like you." Tommy lit another cigarette, took a draw and exhaled, then handed Butch one and lit it for him. "Look, I'm not busting your chops now, alright? I'm giving it to you straight. Same as you did with me in the old days. Think about it. You're a bartender. People like talking to the bartender. You live on this block. Your wife died. She was what, 39? That's young. People are curious, concerned even. Believe me, no one is suspicious. No one's giving you the business. They're just people, being people."

Butch said nothing, still looking unconvinced.

"You've had a rough go. This will all pass. You'll see. Keep your shirt on, big guy."

"Even so, I'll tell you right now. I need a change of scenery. If you hear of some work you think would be a good fit for me, let me know."

Tommy laughed. "You wanna be partners again?"

"Yeah, right. I'd wind up having to kill you," Butch deadpanned. "Before you kill me first."

"There you go. See? You're back to being funny. Keep it up. You're more fun that way. Hey, I'll keep an eye out for some work for you. I gotta shove off. Take care of yourself, my friend."

He was now 41, at a crossroads and on the brink. Overwhelmed, he called Minette for advice.

"Good to hear your voice, Butch. How are you and the kids holding up?"

"We're getting by. The girls are fine. The boys are starting second grade soon."

"And what about Joan? I always worry about her the most."

"That's actually why I'm calling. You know, you're the only woman left I can turn to about this. What do you think I should do with her? She can't cut it in school. She needs more help than teachers have time for. Carol and Marge can't take care of her forever."

"I guess with Ruth gone, it falls on them."

"It's been on them all along. Ruth worked during the day. She never did much for Joan."

"How old is Joan now?"

"She's 13. Going on 6. If someone isn't home to keep an eye on her, she wanders off."

"Aren't one of the other girls home when you're working or are they in school?"

"Marge is. Not Carol. She dropped out three years ago to take care of Joan and the twins."

My mother's last days of school at age 15.
(1942 Rufus King High School yearbook photo)

"Oh my, I didn't know that, Butch."

"She's dating now. Marge, too. I *want* them to have fun. They've earned it, with everything they've been through. I hate to hold them down, you know. But I can't deal with Joan. Don't have the patience. Never have."

"Have you talked to the pastor at St. Casimir's? Maybe he can…"

"Hold it. Stop right there. I'm not asking a man with a collar for advice anymore. I've heard a few vice squad stories about priests that would curl your toes."

"Well, have you contacted Milwaukee Catholic Social Services? I know the director there. In fact, he goes to my church. Whatever options there are for Joan, he'd know."

"What's the guy's name?"

"Bob Johnson. Let me give you his number. Tell him I'm your sister."

———————

He met with Bob and learned of two potential facilities for Joan. One was in Milwaukee, the Lakeside Children's Center on Prospect Avenue. Formerly known for six decades as the Milwaukee Orphans Asylum, the facility had been renamed three years earlier to broaden their identity as a resource for developmentally disabled children. The second facility Bob recommended was out of town.

"In my opinion, the Saint Coletta Home for Exceptional Children is the best fit for your girl. It's run by the Sisters of Saint Francis, although it's an hour away in Jefferson. They're regarded as having one of the best facilities of its kind in the country."

"I've heard of it," Butch acknowledged. "But since Lakeside's local, that would be more practical right now. I'll look into it."

When the traditional school year began, Joan started in a part-time program at Lakeside. By year's end, Butch's public servant experience helped him get a job as a fireman. He now worked the late shift at the Mill Road station house serving Milwaukee's Havenwoods neighborhood on the far north side.

As spring approached in 1947, a phone call from his old pal changed everything.

"Hey, Butch, how are you doing?"

"What's up, Tommy?"

"I ran across another work possibility, if you're interested."

"Is it another barkeep job in bumfuck nowhere?"

"Ha, nice to hear you're keeping your sense of humor."

"Sorry, I know you're looking out for me. Since last we talked, I started working at a firehouse here in town."

"Oh, well, that's good, then. Maybe you wouldn't be interested."

"Go ahead. What is it?"

"It's unbelievable. So, get this. I got this guy that helps me fence cars and parts out west. I'm out there last night. We're talking. The guy happens to mention the police chief there wants out. The town's going to start looking for a replacement soon. So, what do you think? How's that for a tip?"

"What, me? Chief?"

"Hey, why not? All I ask is, look the other way with my car guy there if you get the job. He's a friend. I do good business with him."

"Hell, they'll want a local guy, anyway. Where's this again?"

"Jefferson."

27.

HAIL TO THE CHIEF

Thursday. March 20. Butch donned the suit he last wore for Ruth's funeral and drove to Jefferson to meet with the city's mayor, Ed Rindfleisch. They met at the small police department office off Main Street, joined by Acting Police Chief, Herbert West.

"Mr. Beecher, I have no doubt that you are qualified for the job," stated the mayor. "If you are serious about pursuing this, you will have to appear before City Council members. It would be a group interview. Also, there's the matter of compensation for you as a full-time police chief, which the City Council would also have to approve. I doubt your pay would be what you were accustomed to with the force in Milwaukee. Are you interested in moving forward?"

"Yes. I'm open to working that out. Frankly, the opportunity to enroll one of my daughters at St. Coletta's is a major consideration. I'm offering my services. In exchange for the opportunity, being here would be of tremendous benefit to my family."

"I see. Well, we would certainly welcome your family. Our community is very proud of the work they do at St. Coletta's."

"One other consideration. Ideally, I would like to avoid pulling up stakes 'til my kids' school year ends. Would you be open to that timetable?"

"It's up to you, Herb. Do you mind staying on-duty for a few more months?" the mayor asked his current chief.

"Sure. Whatever it takes to make this work. After all, chances are, Mr. Beecher, I'll still be staying on as a part-time deputy. Are *you* okay with *that*?"

"Can't imagine why I wouldn't be," Butch replied.

The three exchanged handshakes, and the wheels were set in motion. It took time for council members to warm to the idea of hiring a peace officer from the big city, in spite of experience. It would be breaking with precedent on two fronts. Past and present chiefs had all been Jefferson County residents. Chief of Police had always been an elected position. Appointment of an outsider to the chief position could be controversial.

In April, Butch appeared before the City Council for a full interview. Then, on Thursday, May 19, the council held a special meeting for citizens to comment on their proposed hiring. With Butch in attendance, a citizen in the front row rose to speak.

"No offense to you, Mr. Beecher, but police chief has always been an elected position. Shouldn't we hold a special election to fill the post democratically?"

Before the mayor could respond, a second citizen spoke up. "I find it hard to believe that a new chief couldn't be found in Jefferson, or certainly in Jefferson County. How thoroughly have you searched for candidates?"

"Those are fair questions," Mayor Rindfleisch stated. "However, this is a unique circumstance and opportunity to bring on a highly qualified man while saving the time and cost involved to seek out other candidates or to hold a special election."

Butch rose to his feet. "Mr. Mayor, if I may?"

Mayor Reindfleish nodded. Butch turned to face the thirty or so Jeffersonians in attendance.

"I respect both of the concerns that have been voiced. I would feel the same way if I were you. I can only tell you that I would be honored to ply my fourteen years of policing experience in service to this community. My wife passed away last year. It's been a difficult time for me and my five children. Bringing them to Jefferson would be a fresh start for my family. Jefferson is home to one of the finest schools of its kind in the country, Saint Coletta's. I have a daughter with mental disabilities. Living here with all of you while having my daughter nearby at Saint Coletta's would be a blessing for me and my family. I hope you will grant me that blessing. Thank you."

Silence fell over the room as Butch sat down, followed by a smattering of sniffles coming from several women brought to tears by the speech they had just heard.

"Thank you, Mr. Beecher," the mayor said. "Are there any other comments or concerns?"

Silence prevailed until the man in the front row rose again. "I withdraw my concern. I think Mr. Beecher would not only be a fine chief but a fine addition to our community."

Spontaneous applause flowered. Mayor Rindfleisch gaveled the meeting back to order and glanced at the eight council members, four to his left, four to his right.

"All in favor, say aye."

"Aye," came the unanimous response.

"Mr. Beecher, please come forward to be sworn in by the City Clerk," the mayor requested.

Following the meeting, a couple who attended was enjoying a warm spring evening walk home when they saw Butch in his car, just after he turned onto Highway 18 for his drive east to Milwaukee. A familiar German refrain blared from a polka station playing on his car radio, their new chief steering with one hand, while swinging an invisible beer stein in the other:

Ein Prosit, ein Prosit, Der Gemütlichkeit
Ein Prosit, ein Prosit, Der Gemütlichkeit!

When he arrived home, Butch gathered his five children in their living room.

"I've got some news. I want all of you to hear it at the same time. We are moving to Jefferson. You're looking at the new Chief of Police for the City of Jefferson."

His slack-jawed quintet stared back at him in disbelief.

"I worked things out, so we won't move until school's out in June. It's a nice little town. You're going to love it there."

Carol and Marge shrieked simultaneously: *Oh my God! . . . You're kidding . . . Unbelievable!* They jumped up to hug their father. Joan, and the twins joined to form a hug and howl hexagon.

"Wow, all I can say is, I can't wait to get out of here," Carol proclaimed, her voice shaking with emotion at the prospect of extricating herself from the place her stepmother tormented her.

That evening, they peppered their father with question after question about what their future might hold. The next day, Carol and Marge led Joan and the twins in a walk to the North Avenue Library, viewing any book they could find with information, pictures and maps of their soon-to-be new hometown.

For Carol, the spring of 1947 was transformational. Not only did she turn twenty-one, not only was she about to start a new life in a place she had never been to, she was in love. His name was Richard. He lived at his father's house just six blocks east on Bremen Street. At age 23, the lanky, handsome son of a Polish immigrant was like millions of men after World War II, glad to be alive and looking for love. Marge put things in perspective.

"Oh, you're moving with me to Jefferson, alright. We *have* to be together for this adventure. If Richard really wants you, a one-hour drive won't stop him."

47.

NEW POLICE CHIEF—Carroll A. Beecher, Milwaukee, recently appointed chief of police at Jefferson to succeed Herbert West, is a former member of the Milwaukee police force, on which he served 15 years. He is a native of Milwaukee and graduated from St. Thomas' school there. Mr. Beecher is a widower and the father of five children. He plans to move with his family to Jefferson to live permanently.

(Janesville Gazette – May 1947)

28.

WHEELS OF FORTUNE

July 1. They left their densely populated neighborhood in the thirteenth largest city in America with a population of 587,000. Their new home was fifty-two miles west, via State Highways 190 and 18, on the northern outskirts of Jefferson, Wisconsin. Population, 3,000.

The Beechers' new life took root in a country setting at 1009 Marion Street. Their two-story, white-sided house was flanked by huge maple trees, with a long dirt driveway, four times wider than the concrete slivers that sliced through big city lots.

"I don't think I've ever felt so alive," Carol said to Marge as they explored their new world, walking west to Highway 26, the main road into Jefferson where its name changed to Main Street.

Marge brimmed with anticipation. "Dad said if we keep going past the highway, we'll find the Rock River." Along the riverbank, they sat on its grassy edge to bask in nature's beauty. Sunlight glistened atop the river as ducks glided by. They raised a hand to shade their eyes. A tender sprinkle of bird tweets and the flutter of tree frogs blended with the sound of the water's gentle flow. A sense of calm cascaded through them, from skin to soul. Without getting wet, two city girls found themselves rebaptized into new lives and womanhood.

"I love it here. It's so quiet and peaceful. It's like we finally made it over the rainbow," Carol said wistfully. "The green is greener. The sky is bluer."

Marge and Carol in 1947 – Outside their new home in Jefferson, Wisconsin.
(Kortmann family photo, photographer unknown)

When they returned home, Marge gave Joan something to look forward to. "The ducks hopped up from the river and walked right past us like they weren't even afraid. I'll take you there tomorrow to see for yourself."

"Can you take me to see my new school?" Joan asked, perhaps more interested in going the opposite direction to St. Coletta's.

The next day, they did both. After viewing the river, Marge walked a counterclockwise, rectangular street route with Joan to the St. Coletta complex. As they walked the entry road into the wooded campus, several buildings came into view.

"Wow, I think you're going to like going here," Marge told Joan. "Dad said there are a lot of kids that come here who are just like you. The sisters here are very understanding. You can learn at your own pace."

"I want to keep going. Let's go inside," Joan replied.

"We can't do that, Joanie. Not today. Dad made plans to bring you here next week. They'll be expecting you. You'll get a nice tour to see everything inside," assured Marge.

On Monday July 28, Joan spent her first day there. Many of the children there came from far away homes in states across the country to learn and live. Joan was among the fortunate few who lived close enough to return home each day.

Carol's hopes were realized. Throughout July, Richard wrote letters to her nearly every day. A gifted artist, Richard attended Layton School of Art in Milwaukee. Beginning in August, he made weekend day trips to be with Carol. She'd pack a picnic basket, and the two would ride off in Richard's Honolulu Blue Buick Roadmaster Coupe, in search of romantic spots to spend time together. Sometimes, he pulled an easel and paint supplies from the car trunk to reproduce the picturesque scenery on canvas. Butch liked Richard. After several visits, he expressed his rising approval to Carol.

"Seems like he had good brought-ups," he quipped. "If he wants to stay over into Sunday, it's okay by me if he sleeps on the couch in the parlor. As long as you're in your bed upstairs. No monkey business, *verstehen*?"

Meanwhile, Marge discovered being the daughter of a small-town police chief had unique benefits. On the morning of her

August birthday, her father announced, "I've got some stops to make around town. Come with me. I'll give you a first-class tour and introduce some locals to my beautiful daughter."

Off they went, inside one of Jefferson's two patrol cars. Butch delighted in introducing his striking nineteen-year-old daughter around town. Along the way, he pulled in for gas at the Sinclair Station on Main Street, coming to a stop after the cherry-topped squad car's tires rolled over the signal hose that set off the bell in the garage – *ding! ding!*

Out trotted a wiry young man. "Good Morning, Chief," he said with an infectious smile. "Fill 'er up?"

"Yes, and check the oil, too, please."

"Yes, sir," the young man said cheerfully. As he stepped to the front of the car to lift the hood, he couldn't help noticing the striking young woman in the front passenger seat. Marge noticed him going about his business like a man who really enjoyed his job. While squeegeeing both sides of the windshield crystal clear, he caught a glimpse of Marge looking at him. He smiled and nodded with polite charm. After servicing the car, the attendant returned to the driver's door.

"The oil was down half a quart, so I topped it off for you, chief. It's on me. Would you like me to just add the gas to your account?"

"Yes, thank you," Butch replied. "Say, I'd like to introduce my daughter, Marge."

"Nice to meet you, Marge. My name's Korty."

"I'm sorry," Marge said. "What's your name, again?"

"It's Korty. That's my nickname. It's short for my last name."

"What's your last name?" Marge queried.

"Kortmann. K-O-R-T-M-A-N-N," he spelled out, punctuated with a wink and a smile.

Marge returned the pleasantry. "Well, nice to meet you, Korty." Her smile and eyes sparkled.

Chief Beecher pulled out of the Sinclair Station. "He seems like a nice young man. Met him once before. They say he's the best baseball player in town. I'd like to judge for myself. Too bad the season is over. I'll have to give him a look next spring."

"He sure has a nice smile," Marge said.

Her father looked at her as he drove. "I know that look."

"What look?"

"You like him. I can tell."

Marge blushed and smiled. They stopped at Bon Ton Bakery on Racine Street where Butch picked out a birthday cake and introduced his daughter.

"Irv, Elsie, this is my second daughter, Margaret," Butch said to the owners, whom he had met several times before. "We're here to pick out a cake for her birthday."

"Well, Happy Birthday, Margaret! It's a pleasure to meet you," Elsie said, with Irv quickly echoing his wife's well wishes.

"I'll take this one," Butch decided while pointing to a white frosted red velvet cake.

"Alright, let me box it right up for you, Chief, and tell you what, it's on us. Consider it our birthday gift to you, Margaret," Elsie said happily.

The four exchanged parting pleasantries, and the Beecher's returned to the squad car.

"Time to head back home. I'm going to work late tonight. Let's have lunch with your brothers and sisters. I'll sing you a Happy Birthday, so I can get a piece of that nice cake before I go."

"Sounds wonderful," Marge answered. "Thanks for the tour. It sure is nice having a police chief for a dad." She winked and gave him a big hug.

Later that afternoon, Marge told Carol, "I think I met someone."

"What? You're kidding!" blurted Carol, with a burst of excitement. "Who is he? Where did you meet him?"

"He works at the Sinclair Station. I barely talked to him. He just had a certain something. A gleam in his eyes."

"What's his name?" Carol asked.

Marge laughed. "Sinclair Man."

"Sinclair Man?" Carol chortled. "Huh?"

"Yeah. He works at the Sinclair gas station. I'm not sure what he said his name was. I think he said it's Korty. It sounded like Corky but I'm pretty sure he said it's Korty. Yes, that's it. It's short for his last name. Kortmann."

"And you hardly talked to him?" Carol wondered. "I'd have never thought you'd get hit by Cupid's arrow at a filling station."

Marge laughed and quipped, "I'll have to get a driver's license, so I can take dad's car in for gas every day."

"So, how do you know he's available? I take it he wasn't wearing a ring?"

"No ring, just a really nice smile. And the way he looked at me. I felt it. I think he did, too. I swear, I could see it in *his* eyes."

29.

CUPIDITY

"I've got it!" Carol proclaimed. "How about this: Richard's driving here on Saturday. We ride with him to the filling station, so I can check out Sinclair Man."

"I'd rather be the one driving the car in," Marge answered.

Carol tilted her head back with brows raised and eye's widened at the audacious idea. "You would do that?"

"Do you think Richard would let me?"

Saturday arrived. So did Marge. After a bit of secret practice driving with Richard, she pulled into the Sinclair station behind the wheel of Richard's Buick. *Ding, ding!* went the bell, signaling her call of seduction. Her heartbeat quickened at the sight of her hoped-for moment unfolding. In her eyes, the *Sinclair Man* trotted out from the overhead door opening, as if her man of destiny were gliding to her in dreamy slow motion. His expression transformed. A look of sublime satisfaction washed over him.

"Wow! It's my lucky day. Nice to see you again, Margaret. Is this your car?"

"Nope, it's his," she replied with a tilt of her head to the man on her right, where Richard was seated at the other end of the front seat. Carol sat between them with a grin like the sun overlooking the glory of morning flower petals opening.

"This is my sister, Carol, and that's her boyfriend, Richard, from Milwaukee."

"You came a long way just to buy some gas," joked Sinclair Man. "Nice to meet you. I'm Korty." Sinclair Man extended his right hand to clasp Richard's with a handshake exchange in front of Carol's face.

"I don't suppose you could drop what you're doing and join us?" Marge asked boldly.

"Well, I can't now, but Lloyd's coming in an hour or so. Can you come back then?"

They did. This time, with Richard at the wheel, Carol to his right and Marge leaning out the left rear window with a gleaming smile of anticipation. Now in street clothes, *Sinclair Man* walked out. Marge opened her door and slid to the right to make room. Slam went that left rear door. Richard drove away with destiny unfolding in his back seat.

Carol accepted Richard's proposal of marriage in November. Her destiny awaited back in her hometown of Milwaukee, where the two planned to marry the following summer.

A month later, the December 27 edition of the Jefferson newspaper proclaimed news of a double betrothal:

Beecher-Kortmann Betrothal

The engagement of Miss Margaret E. Beecher, daughter of Police Chief Carroll Beecher, to Wilbur "Korty" Kortmann, son of Mr. and Mrs. Ed Kortmann, North Main Street, was announced at a dinner at the Beecher house on Christmas Day. It followed the recently announced engagement of another daughter, Carol Beecher, to Richard Sierlecki, 2658 N. Bremen Street, Milwaukee.

Sparky's had quickly become *the* tavern in Jefferson in 1947. Located in the heart of town at the corner of Main and Racine Streets, the longtime watering hole was purchased a year earlier by Franklin "Sparky" Multhauf, a young, local World War II veteran who survived serious injury while fighting in the Pacific theatre in 1943. Naturally, with the city police station and jail in immediate proximity just down the block, it became known as the place where Chief Beecher could unofficially hold court. With each *shot-and-a-beer* round, his law man façade transformed to a more mellow version of his Big Daddy persona of old.

On New Year's Eve, Chief Beecher departed the station in street clothes at 9 p.m., leaving Deputy Ed West in charge. After an hour of lubrication, gregarious Butch was in the midst of telling tales from his days of policing in Milwaukee when two women entered the bar. They paused as they noticed every stool was occupied.

"Come on over, ladies!" he bellowed and rose from his stool. "Get up and give one of the ladies a seat," he said to the stranger seated next to him. "Have some manners, me boyo."

As the two women made their way toward Butch, it seemed everyone but him knew their names.

"Hey, Demi!"

"Hi, Lila!"

"Hello, thank you for the seat. I'm Demi," the first woman said and extended her right hand to shake his, while her female companion stopped to speak with a man two stools down.

Butch's large hand extended to gently envelope hers with a gentlemanly clasp. "I'm Carroll, but you can call me But . . ."

"I *know* who you are, Chief. I've heard good things about you and now I finally get to meet you."

"I see. What good things have you heard?"

"That you are a family man who's been raising five children on his own."

"Well, not really on my own. My wife died two years ago. My older daughters do a lot to pick up the slack. First one's on me. What are you drinking?"

"He knows." Just as Demi responded, barkeep Sparky placed her Old Fashioned on a coaster.

She removed her lime green, wool trench coat. It's high collar and wide lapels exposed the coat's stylish, plaid flannel lining. After removing her wide brimmed hat in matching lime green, she shook out her medium length, dark blonde hair. In a gentlemanly manner, Butch took her coat and hat.

"These are too nice to put onto that coat rack." He carried her coat and hat past the end of the bar and through an 'Employee's Only' doorway. He stepped back to his spot next to Demi. "I put your things on the owner's rack. Classy duds like yours deserve a place of their own." It was Big Daddy's old charm offensive in full flower. Minutes earlier, his story telling had captured the attention of everyone on his end of the bar. Instinctively, his modus operandi for zeroing in on an object of affection moved into high gear. Demi had an elegance about her. She spoke with an uncommon, high-class articulation that left him spellbound. Halfway through her second Old Fashioned, with inhibitions withdrawn, she signaled unambiguously.

"I must say, you are devilishly handsome. More so than I expected," she added with a lilting laugh and sigh.

Once the two-way flirting started, it was a one-way ticket to paradise. Just like that, Butch became the third Beecher bitten by the love bug in six months.

On January 31, 1948, Margaret Beecher married Wilbur "Korty" Kortmann. Butch purchased a new grey suit to escort his second daughter down the aisle of St. Mark's English Lutheran

Church on Sanborn Avenue. On the bride's side of the front row next to Chief Beecher, Demi appeared alongside him in public for the first time. The divorced mother of two teenage girls charmed the newlyweds and his other four children with all the right first impression notes. No mean feat, considering their experience with his last sidekick.

"How about that Demi?" Carol remarked to Marge that night before they parted company.

"I got a good feeling about her right away," said the new Mrs. Kortmann. "With me out of the house now and you going back to Milwaukee in what, six months? The Old Boy might be lining her up for duty."

30.

SISTERLY ADVICE

Unlike his life's chapter with Ruth, the love Butch had for Demi was the real deal. He adored her. With Carol still around to hold down the domestic fort, he felt free to devote his energies to *chiefly* duties and courting his elegant new prize. Perhaps subconsciously, he seemed preoccupied with putting his ten-year mid-life crisis behind him, as if his sentence for past bad choices had been served and he was now free to enjoy the fruits of a new life in Jefferson. He was on a roll and in no mood for distractions.

February.

"Dad, a sister from Saint Coletta called," Carol told her father when he returned home one evening in March. "She wants you to call her tomorrow. I wrote her information on a piece of paper and left it on your dresser."

He went to his bedroom to look at her note – *Sr. Mary Anastasia, Superintendent, 261-0100.* His return phone call the next morning led to an afternoon meeting in the boss nun's office.

"Thank you for coming in, Chief Beecher."

"Please, Sister, call me Carroll."

"I'll meet you in the middle with Mr. Beecher, then," she stickled with a wink.

"Of course."

"Regarding your Joan, she truly is a sweetheart and has never posed any problems. It's just that this semester, it has been evident that she is, well, in a boy-crazy phase."

"That's not really abnormal, is it?"

"No, certainly not. However, three staff members who spend time with her regularly have reported Joan has particular difficulty responding to our usual methods to help girls her age to control her impulses."

"Huh. So, what has she been doing?"

"Things like hugging and kissing some boys, which is not uncommon for girls her age to occasionally do. Her urges are stronger than average. Sometimes, she touches herself during class or during an activity. She's also touched a few boys inappropriately. When we scold her, she tends to not take it seriously. Again, this is not necessarily uncommon. However, since Joan has home privileges, I felt you should know about her high-risk behavior. When it's recognized in our resident students, we take precautions wherever possible to prevent the possibilities of a sexual encounter. Your daughter is one of our few non-resident students. She has an independent streak in her, which is normal and healthy, as it is for any young person progressing toward adulthood. I encourage you to emphasize vigilance with her guardians when she is off campus."

"Alright. What do you suggest I do?"

"I suppose you should do the same thing you would do if you knew any one of your teen daughters tended toward promiscuity. Keep her supervised at all times. Help her avoid temptation. Keep her away from young men and boys her age. Don't be angry with her. Don't threaten her. Just be vigilant."

Butch thanked the superintendent for her time and returned

home. He popped open a bottle of Miller and plopped down with a newspaper. As the evening rolled by and her siblings went to bed, Carol needed her curiosity satisfied.

"What was your meeting with Sister Mary Anastasia about? Anything I should know?"

Her father balked momentarily, having never talked about sexuality with one of his kids. "Long story short, your sister is boy crazy. They just want us to keep as eye on her, you know what I mean?"

"She's never with boys by herself. I'm always with her when she is out. We've talked about boys here and there. I guess the usual girl talk. What should I do? Should I avoid the subject?"

"Hell, yeah! Don't bring it up, and, if she brings it up, tell her it's wrong to think about it and it's wrong to talk about it."

Joan Beecher c. 1948
(Kortmann family photo, photographer unknown)

31.

DISPATCHED

Friday. April 9. One of Marge's favorite movies, *The Adventures of Robin Hood*, was playing at the Jefferson Theatre to celebrate the movie's ten- year anniversary. With husband, Korty, working that evening, she was unaccustomed to going to the movies alone. She had seen the movie twice years earlier in Milwaukee with Carol. Knowing Joan had never seen the movie, she called Joan and offered to treat her to a show.

"It's showing at 7 p.m. Can Dad give you a ride to the theater?"

"I think so."

"Good! How about you get there about ten minutes before? I'll wait for you out front."

Carol had supper ready at 5:30. Butch was working late and would not be joining them. With her father absent, Joan knew she wouldn't have a ride to the theater. She told Carol that Marge promised to treat her to "the Robin Hood movie." At first, Carol refused to let Joan leave without a ride to the movie house a mile and half away. Joan pleaded her case.

"It's not fair. I know where to go. You know I do. I walked that way with you lots of times," she protested and began to cry.

Carol often felt sorry for Joan. She was confident Joan could find her way there. "I'll tell you what. The boys and I will walk with you down to Main Street. Then, all you have to do is walk straight up Main to the theater. But we'll have to leave right now. I'll clean the dishes when I get back." The four departed, walking the half mile north to Main Street. Joan turned left and started the mile walk up into town. Carol turned around to head back home with Jim and John. As Carol washed the supper dishes, the phone rang at 7:20 p.m.

"Hey, it's me. I've been waiting for Joan here at the theater. Dad should've dropped her off by now."

"No, Dad is working tonight. Joan should have been there by now. I walked her down to Main Street, and she was sure she knew her way straight up Main. She should have been there at least half an hour ago."

"Hmmm, I don't like the sound of that," Marge said ominously. "I'll look around for her. I wonder if she stopped in the park or maybe she went to the hamburger stand. You know how she likes both of those places."

"Check at the Sinclair, too. Maybe she stopped there to see Korty," Carol added.

Marge's search proved fruitless. In a desperate panic, she ran south on Main Street and rushed into the police station. "Dad! Joan is missing. She was supposed to meet me at the theater and she never showed up. Something is wrong. I'm afraid something is terribly wrong!"

"What do you mean she was supposed to meet you at the theater? She's not supposed to be walking around out on her own, God dammit!"

"Aaaa, I don't know. I didn't know she isn't supposed to be out on her own. She knows her way around."

He cocked his head, his face set with penetrating eyes and pursed lips that spoke volumes in angry silence. Rolling in his chair to his left, he radioed Deputy West.

"10-18, Herb, 10-18."

"Copy, Chief. West here, over."

"10-18, we have a missing fifteen-year-old girl, about five feet tall, very thin build, dark brown hair. Last seen in the area of the railroad tracks on North Main Street, walking south to the movie theater. Stop what you're doing and start rolling through every street in town from north to south. Look for her and anything that looks suspicious. Copy."

"10-4, Chief. 10-4"

"Copy that, Herb. I'm calling in Larry to cover dispatch, so I can patrol downtown on foot, over."

"10-4"

Butch rolled his chair back to face Marge. "Go back out and stand in front of the theater. When Larry gets here, I'll come join you. We'll search inside the theater and then I'll walk you home." He phoned home and let Carol know Joan was missing and told her to call the station immediately if Joan showed up at the house.

———————————

11:30 p.m. Joan entered the Beecher house. Carol jumped from a chair she occupied near the phone. "Joan, thank God. Where were you?"

"I met a friend at the theater. We were together for a while, and then she walked me back home."

"Oh, God, everyone was worried sick about you. Have a seat here with me while I call Dad to let him know you're back." Carol called the station and informed Deputy Ruehl.

"Keep her right there, Carol. I'll get word to your father. He'll be there as soon as he can."

Saturday 12:15 a.m. Butch arrived home. Carol sensed the need to reassure him immediately. "She's alright. Please don't be upset with her."

"Where the hell were you?"

"I went to the theater. I found a friend. After the show, she walked back here with me."

"Marge was there. You never showed up. Where were you all this time?

Joan shrugged, "I told you." She looked down nervously.

"I'm not buying it," he growled, shaking his head, a scowl of contempt. "Get the hell upstairs. We'll talk about this again in the morning."

Saturday 6:00 a.m. The phone rang several times in the Beecher house. Butch answered "Chief Beecher, speaking."

"Chief, this is Deputy Sheriff Conlon, Fort Atkinson. Wanted you to know we are holding a suspect here on suspicion of theft in Lake Koshkonong. His name is Arvin Hill, alias James Fraser. We tracked him down to the Wisconsin Hotel in Jefferson, where he was registered under the alias. His alibi is he was in Jeff all night. I'm hoping you can come interrogate him and help us verify his whereabouts."

Butch drove to Fort Atkinson. He was greeted by Deputy Sheriff Conlon, who took the Chief to an interrogation room. Conlon stepped out and returned moments later with the handcuffed suspect.

"What has he told you, so far?" Butch asked Conlon.

"He was over your way, in a tavern and a hotel. That's it."

"Let me talk to him," Butch said to Conlon, who gestured with his arm, as if to say, *go ahead*. "Alone, please."

"Sure," replied Conlon. He pulled the door shut as he exited and walked down the hallway to chat with a fellow deputy.

No more than a minute later, the deputies heard yelling and the sound of furniture crashing from inside the interrogation room. Conlon rushed back down the hall. Before he could open the door, Butch opened it from the inside. He stepped out, slightly out of breath. "The son-of-a-bitch confessed. Record his goddamn statement. Rape and larceny." In a corner behind him, the moaning suspect was curled in a heap. Conlon nodded. The deputies brushed by to check on the suspect while the visiting chief picked up his hat and retightened his tie.

Saturday 9:00 a.m. Butch returned home and confronted his daughter. "It was a man, wasn't it? Joan stiffened and said nothing. "WASN'T IT!?" he yelled. Cowering, Joan recoiled defensively, muted by terror. "Go upstairs and stay in your room, goddammit." Joan began to sob as she headed to the staircase. "I want her in that room 'til I come back," he barked at Carol as he headed out the door.

An hour later, he returned with Jefferson physician, Arthur Robinson. The two men went upstairs to Joan's room. "This is Doctor Robinson," Butch informed his daughter. "He's going to take a look at you. When he asks a question, you give him an answer." Butch left the room and went below.

Ten minutes later, the doc came downstairs. "Well Chief, I can't tell with absolute certainly that she was raped, but based on what she told me, it sure sounds like a sexual assault."

Saturday 2:30 p.m. Butch drove with Joan to the Jefferson County Sheriff's Department in Fort Atkinson, where Arvin Hill had been transferred. Walking with his hand around his daughter's skinny left arm, a deputy sheriff guided them into the jail section, where they stopped in front of the cell where suspect Hill sat. "Stand up,"

Chief Beecher ordered. He looked at Joan, "Is this the man you were with last night?" Appearing frightened by her surroundings and on the verge of tears, she looked up at her father, her face wracked by fear. "Is this who you were with last night?" Butch pressed, his voice raised. Joan nodded. "If it is, say yes."

"Yes."

Tuesday, April 13. A story was published in the Janesville Gazette about an arrest in connection with an alleged rape incident involving a 14-year-old Jefferson girl. Chief Beecher was named twice in the article, which also stated the girl positively identified her assailant at the Jefferson County jail. Readers had no idea the victim was the 15-year-old developmentally disabled daughter of the city's police chief.

Monday, April 19, 8:00 a.m.

Butch came out of his main floor bedroom in full Chief Beecher dress. "Time to go. Do you have everything packed?"

"I guess," Carol replied reluctantly.

Out he went with the suitcase. He stowed it in his car trunk and returned inside. "Let's go." A minute later he pulled away with Joan to his right in the front seat.

Arrest Is Made in Rape Case

North Dakota Man Is Identified in Attack on Jefferson Girl

Jefferson—Arvid Hill, 27, Fargo, N. D., waived preliminary hearing when he appeared this afternoon before Justice William Brandel on a charge of rape involving a 14-year old girl. He was bound over to circuit court and placed under $5,000 bond. Hill was returned to county jail to await trial. The alleged assault occurred in Jefferson Friday evening, according to Dist. Atty. Francis Garity. Hill signed a confession for Dist. Atty. Garity Tuesday morning in the presence of Sheriff Roland Gibson and Police Chief Carroll Beecher.

Anticipating a guilty plea, Chief Beecher stated that authorities hoped to have Hill in the state penitentiary at Waupun by the end of the week. The child was examined by Dr. Arthur Robinson who confirmed her story of rape. The girl also identified her assailant in Jefferson county jail.

Police picked up Hill for questioning Saturday morning in connection with larceny at the Gustaveson farm, Lake Koshkonong. He told police that he had come to Jefferson from Fort Atkinson Friday evening, attended a movie, visited several taverns, and then spent the night at the Wisconsin hotel where he registered under the name of James Fraser.

Mrs. Russell Baumgard identified Hill as the man who had been in the Baumgard tavern after 11 p. m. Friday.

The crime carries a penalty of up to 35 years imprisonment.

"Where are we going?" she asked.

It took him a few seconds to respond. "You need to be where someone can always keep an eye on you."

He drove past the usual left turn onto County Highway Y toward Saint Coletta's. Fear overtook Joan's apprehension as the car's speed increase and unfamiliar countryside filled her view. "You passed my school. Where are we going?"

"I already told you. It's a place where people can keep a good eye on you. They'll take good care of you."

"That's what they were doing at Saint Coletta's. I liked it there. Why are we going somewhere else?"

"Because what you did when you went off with that man was inexcusable. I can't let that happen again."

"But you do bad things, too."

His eyes momentarily left the road to glare her way. "You don't know what you're talking about."

"I don't even know if you love me. Not like you do with Carol and Marge."

"You have no idea what love is."

"Yes, I do. I loved mama. She was sad about Baby Danny. You made her sad, too."

"Shut up! You don't know what you're talking about. And don't say things like that. No one's going to believe you, anyway."

She gave him the stink eye.

He turned on the car's radio, pressed the lighter button and pulled open the ash tray. "You can't be trusted. I can't trust you. Your sisters can't trust you. I know you can't help yourself. You don't know any better." *Ching* went the heated lighter, punctuating his words. *Crackle* went his cellophaned pack of Kool's as he raised it from pocket to mouth, shaking one loose to clasp between his lips. He lit his cigarette, popped the lighter back in its home and turned up the radio volume. Surrealness enveloped their ride. For the next hour, the blare of a radio station broadcast squelched conversation. He cracked the driver door window open periodically, venting some of the smoke but none of the tension. Their ride came to an end in front of a long, window-filled, two-and-a-half story structure, with a presence not unlike the main entrance structures of Saint Coletta's.

"This is it. Let's go," declared Butch. They walked side-by-side toward an entrance guarded by two white columns stretching up to the triple-arched portico that dwarfed the two glass entry doors. He announced their arrival to a woman at a reception desk. They sat together on one of several unoccupied, long wooden benches. After a few minutes, two white-cloaked, male orderlies entered, veiled with welcoming faces as they approached the mustachioed law man seated next to the anxious waif beside him. Butch rose with a hand gesture, summoning his daughter to rise. He looked down at her, extending his right arm across her shoulders. "This is your new home. They'll take good care of you here."

"Welcome, Joan," said the orderly closest to her, his arm gently extending across her shoulders in symbolic transition as Butch's arm withdrew. "Come with us, please, won't you?"

Her frail body tightened. She turned to clutch her father's overcoat. He pulled away and looked at one of the men. "Take her in. I'll be right back."

"No! No, no, no!" Joan shrieked. She scuffled passively as the men guided her to the door they came from, her father's ears undoubtedly taking in the commotion behind him. He reentered a minute later and dropped the suitcase at the reception desk before heading out for good.

Joan had just become the newest inmate of The Southern Wisconsin Colony and Training School, most commonly referred to as Southern Colony, a state-funded mental institution in Union Grove, Wisconsin. One week earlier, on the first business day after her "crime," her father filed commitment paperwork in Jefferson County's Juvenile Court. By week's end, a judge had sealed her fate.

****

In documents I obtained in 2016, residents of Southern Colony back then were, indeed, labeled in official records as inmates, not patients, a reflection of the facility's history since its inception under the jurisdiction of Wisconsin's Department of Corrections.

The text of my grandfather's statement regarding the event that triggered her commitment reads, as follows:

> "On the night of April 9th, Joan evaded the 19-year-old married sister who attempted to call for her at the movie and came walking home while the family and sheriff's deputies were looking for her. She explained she had walked home with a girlfriend she had met. The next morning, the father, as Jefferson Chief of Police, detained a disheveled hitchhiker, wanted by a county farmer on a felony charge. Questioning revealed that he had struck up an acquaintance with Joan in the theater, had walked her home by a devious route and had raped her in a field on a dead-end street. Joan finally admitted these facts."

During my research of police involved incidents in Jefferson in 1948, current city officials informed me that police reports no longer existed from that era. Online newspaper archives were the one source I found that offered insight. Aside from the rape incident, I was able to find four additional articles involving the Jefferson Police Department that were published that year: a minor girl eloped to Milwaukee in January without her parents' permission, four minors were arrested for drinking in August, a woman hanged herself in her home in September, a new ordinance against dogs at large was enacted in December. In the context of crimes in a small town, some may have viewed the rape of a local girl as the city's most heinous incident that year. It's likely those denizens asked around, curious to learn who the victim was.

32.

FACTOR OF THREE

Rather than drive straight to the Jefferson police station, the chief stopped at home. Once inside, he saw Marge had come to join Carol for lunch. It was apparent from his daughter's reddened eyes that the two had been crying.

"What's wrong?" he asked.

"We were just talking about Joan," Carol said. Minutes earlier, she'd told Marge about the suitcase of Joan's belongings she had packed at their father's request nearly four hours earlier. Butch could readily see that his oldest daughters were struggling to process their sister's unannounced exodus from their lives.

"I took her to an institution in Union Grove called Southern Colony. I had no choice. It's for her own good."

"How long will she be there?" asked Marge.

"I don't know. Maybe for good. You have to face up to reality. It's where she belongs."

Marge broke into tears and shook her head. "It's our fault. I should've known better than to invite her to that movie."

"I feel to blame, too," Carol whimpered. "I should have never let her leave the house."

"Forget about it. I don't want to hear that talk. This was bound to happen with your sister sooner or later. It wasn't the first time she disappeared without telling anyone. She's at the age where I can't control her anymore. None of us can."

"Can we visit her?" Marge asked.

"I don't know," her father replied while slapping a sandwich together. "Maybe someday. It's her new home now. She needs to get used to it without us. You need to get used to it, too. Don't worry about her. You have a husband to think about now. They'll take good care of her there."

He left the kitchen and returned ten minutes later in street clothes, having shed the official armor that helped him detach from the odious nature of the task he'd just completed.

"I'm heading to the station. I'll be home late."

"What should I tell the boys?" asked Carol, wondering how he wanted Joan's absence explained to his nine-year-old sons.

"Tell 'em the truth. Just tell them what I just told you. Don't make a big deal about it. Tell them she'll be happier there. Make it sound positive. Because it is, for everyone involved."

In June, twins Jim and John finished third grade. Carol sent out wedding invitations, mostly to Richard's family members in Milwaukee.

Meanwhile, in Union Grove, their sister completed her seventh week of institutional captivity. In her first days there, medical staff examined her and documented their assessment:

> "White female, 14 years, 4 months of age, about average height (5' 1.5"); slender and underweight; weighing 89.5 pounds. Poor physical development. History of congenital syphilis. Frontal bosses on head. 4 teeth missing. 2 teeth have fillings. 2 other teeth have

temporary fillings. Asymmetry of face and chest. Left side of face smaller than opposite side. Right side of chest smaller anterior and larger posterior than opposite side. Scoliosis to right of dorsal spine. Abdominal lordosis. Right arm and leg smaller than opposite members. Reflexes right arm and leg exaggerated. Pupils are irregular and unequal; left is larger; pupils do not react to light and accommodation. Lateral strabismus of left eye. Laboratory report: Serological test for syphilis on blood specimen was POSITIVE 3 plus.

Joan's last menstrual period is stated as April 8th and April 12th, but she has not menstruated since, nor has she menstruated since coming to our institution on April 19, 1948.

The provisional diagnosis is borderline mental deficiency; congenital syphilis with involvement of the central nervous system. Observation for possible pregnancy.

We are advised that she had some treatment including 'shock treatment,' but we are unable to verity the treatment or amount of treatment."

As time passed, it was apparent that Joan was not pregnant. No rape testing was indicated; rape kits did not exist until the 1970's. In Joan's eighth week at Southern Colony, she entered the facility's hospital. She began receiving treatments of penicillin and other drugs with the goal of eradicating her congenital syphilis.

Two months later, Carol became Mrs. Richard Sierlecki on August 7 at St. Casimir's Church on Bremen Street in Milwaukee, located two blocks south of where Richard lived with his father, sisters and stepmother. The day was charged with happiness and high emotion, not only for the bride, but for Marge, as well. Their sisterly bond forever entwined from weathering every challenge together since childhood. The twins attended with their father, who was now accompanied regularly by his lady friend of seven months, Demi. Topped with a stylish, wide-brimmed hat, she and the father-of-the-bride may have been the most fashionable pair of guests on Carol's most joyous day.

Front L-to-R: John and Jim Beecher.
Behind L-to-R: Bride Carol, Carroll, Demi and her daughter.
(Kortmann family photo, photographer unknown)

"I don't remember ever seeing the Old Boy this happy," Marge remarked to Carol in a private moment during the reception at nearby Polish Falcon's Hall. "He never looked that happy with Ruth. Not for a single day."

"She's good for him," Carol said. "I'm glad. She's great with John and Jim. She'll be taking over for me, helping to raise them. I'd bet on it."

Her words were prophetic, albeit not entirely surprising. In need of someone to mother his children, both Carol and Marge had seen their father's courtship dance before. His previous choice for the role of wife-mother-homemaker was an act of both desperation and necessity. At least this time, his affection for Demi appeared genuine to the two young women who were there for it all. Ten days later, Marge telephoned Carol with word of changes in the offing.

"I've got the scoop for you Mrs. S." Marge quipped. "Demi's moving in with Dad, but not at Marion Street. They're moving downtown into a big apartment in the Puerner Building, that long two-story place on Main.

"You're kidding! Really? It's such a nice house. Why would he leave it for an apartment?"

"I guess Demi didn't really care for the house. When she heard the renter of the two-bedroom over Sparky's was moving, she wanted it, insisted on it, actually."

"Ah ha! It's above Sparky's? That's why the Old Boy went along with it," Carol concluded.

"Yep. In a way, it makes sense when you think about it," Marge replied. "He can walk to the station, now. The boys walk to school is a lot shorter. Plus, Demi will be closer to her sister's house."

"And he'll be closer to his favorite tavern now than he was on Richard's Street," Carol noted. "I didn't think that was possible. So, I take it they're getting married?"

"Demi told me they've talked about it, but it's not a priority right now. The landlord at the apartment said they had to move in September 1st, in order to get the place. She's busy getting ready to move out of her sister's place and helping with all the packing at Dad's."

With September's arrival, the latest iteration of the Beecher family began residing at 912 ½ Main St. When the twins turned ten at the end of October, Demi's sister Lila came to their apartment to help celebrate. After the boys were off to bed, Lila offered a bit of cocktail fueled candor. "Far be it for me to tell you two what to do." She looked at Butch. "You might not be as accustomed to the buzz in a small town like Demi and I are. People talk. On more than one occasion, I've been asked if you two married or if you are *living in sin.*"

"I know how people talk. I had my fill of *busy bodies* in Milwaukee. It's nobody's goddamn business what I do in my personal life."

"Now Carroll, think about it. Lila has a point," countered Demi, addressing him by his formal name. She found his nickname unbecoming, eschewing it for his birth name since the start of their relationship. "People have high expectations for their police chief, right down to morality in his personal life. Let's face it. It's about time we get married."

"Is that a proposal?"

"In more ways than one. It's the right thing for us *and* your job."

On December 23, Chief Carroll Beecher married Demi Clark in a courthouse ceremony with four of his five children present.

****

1948. A seminal year for the Beechers. Three weddings. A third wife for their patriarch. It was his first full year as a police chief. He gave away three daughters.

(Photo credit unknown)

33.

PAST IS PROLOGUE

"Whereof what's past is prologue;
what to come, in yours and my discharge."
~Antonio in William Shakespeare's, The Tempest (c. 1611)

1949. As his decade of tumult drew to a close, autumn's beauty colored Butch's world in unprecedented fashion. He became a grandfather twice in a forty-five-day span. Marge gave birth to a son in September. She named him Daniel, to honor the name her father gave his first son in 1934. The next month, Carol had a son. He was named Victor. Coincidentally, he was born October 31, the same date his young uncles were born 11 years earlier.

Unlike his years of discontent with wife number two, his eldest daughters could not recall the last time their father looked truly happy beside his wife. Born Delma Hildegard Anderson, the Scandinavian blond was six years his junior, mindful of her figure, with a waft of sophistication that bordered on haughty. She took great pride in each of her new roles. To help raise her stepsons, her maternal warmth filled the void left by the departure of their three *sister-mothers* the previous year. Her view of wifely duties bore the quaint romanticism of bygone nobility. "I'm old-fashioned," she admitted decades later. "I still believe the man is king of the castle. The wife's job is to be his queen, keep her king happy and make their home a castle." For Butch, his third time was the proverbial charm. At least, it appeared that way.

Though young wife Marge now had a Jefferson life of her own, she visited her nearby brothers regularly. Her sense of duty after years of prematurely honing her own motherly instincts in her teens would remain undiminished for the rest of her life. Demi's place in her life was a blessing. Her new stepmother modeled duty and commitment, both in the way she opened her heart to her stepsons and in the manner she carried herself publicly, as wife of the city's number one role model. Their unspoken, mutual respect allowed conversation between them to flow with equal comfort.

"You're just so joyful, Marge. Your spirit helps me feel young again. Has your father ever told you about my wild times when I was your age?"

"To tell you the truth, since I've been married, we haven't talked much at all. He's got you now, and I've got Korty. We both have our hands full now," joked Marge with a laugh.

"Oh, my. Well, when I was eighteen, even younger than you are now, I had to get away from here. I couldn't wait to see what life was like in a big city. I couldn't wait to head off to Chicago. Those were such glamorous times, don't you know," mused Demi as she sat in wistful pose, clutching and caressing her pearls as she always did, while enunciating *dontcha know*, in deliberate violation of *Wisconsinese*.

"Wow. So, you moved there all on your own?"

"Not exactly. My cousin Magnus lived there at the time, so I had a place to stay. First, I worked as a waitress. Once I got my feet wet, the night life was like nothing else! Good looking men were everywhere," she sighed, dreamily. "I never had to buy my own drink, and I was quite the dancer, don't you know."

"So, you were one of those flappers," Marge speculated, familiar with the mystique of liberated women in the Roaring Twenties, before the term "women's lib" carved its way into American lexicon and Westernized cultures around the world five decades later.

Demi laughed, "Oh, that and more, my dear. If you must know, I made a living for a few years as a burlesque dancer."

"Really?" Marge blushed in amazement.

"Oh, yes, the stories I could tell you," Demi ruminated. "Just between you and me, that's my secret with your father. I can get him to do most anything I want by dancing for him. I can't imagine what a rascal he was back in those days."

"Ha, I wouldn't know, but I'd be lying if I said I hadn't noticed he's always been quite the lady-killer."

As sisters will do, Marge couldn't wait to chat with Carol and to share her stepmother's sizzling morsels.

"Oh, boy. *Kitzel!*" Carol roiled playfully over revelations about Demi's sexually charged past, using one of the many German expressions their father uttered with periodically. "The Old Boy really found his match alright. I hate to say it, but looking back on it, I don't see how our mother was ever his type."

"She was a doll when they married. Of course, she was his type, physically anyway," Marge replied. "Mom was demure. To a fault. Ruth was a real operator. In the worst ways. Demi has a knack. She plays everything, just right."

Sisters talk. Whether by blood, or at heart, or oath to Jesus, when trust is high, they can talk about anything. Even the Sisters of Saint Francis of Assisi. Even at a place like Saint Coletta's, mercy's ground zero.

Word trickled out about one of its newest residents, a 31-year-old woman from Massachusetts. Her name was Rosemary Kennedy, the daughter of high-powered businessman, political figure and former U.S. Ambassador to the United Kingdom, Joseph P. Kennedy. It was rumored Rosemary suffered permanent brain damage from a failed frontal lobotomy year's earlier, an experimental procedure intended to reduce her learning difficulties and periodic outbursts of angry frustration. Rosemary's issues were similar to Joan Beecher's, at least they were before her father gambled with her life.

Whispers about the daughter of a locally prominent father also made their way from Saint Coletta's into Jefferson:

> *The chief's daughter disappeared after that rape happened last year . . . why did he send her away to a mental institution . . . why wouldn't he place her in the custody of Coletta's nuns . . . was she really raped . . . did he make up the crime as an excuse to send her away for good?*

———————————

1950. Marge was now licensed to drive. Legally. She took a ride with her infant son to Milwaukee to visit Carol, who was pregnant again. While the baby boys crawled and babbled, their mothers talked.

"Demi still stops by a few times every week when the boys are in school. Does she still call you regularly?"

"She calls every so often, not every week, though. More like once, maybe twice a month. It's nice that she calls. She asks how I'm doing, how Victor is doing and about Richard."

"Well, she's asked me twice lately about dad and his nightmares. She asked me if he had nightmares in the past. Has she talked to you about that?"

"No. What did you tell her?"

"I told her he'd have them every so often, that we could hear him shout himself awake from our room upstairs. She asked how often it would happen. I said it's been a long time. Probably since we moved from 26th Street to Richards Street. At least a couple of times a year, maybe more."

"Why do you think she's been asking about it?"

"It sounds like the nightmares are happening more often. Demi said sometimes he wakes her up and scares the heck out of her, yelling things out while he's still sleeping. Sometimes, he sits up screaming like he's terrified. She said she has to yell at him and shake him to wake him up."

"Has she asked him what his nightmares are about?" Carol wondered.

"Yes, but he won't talk about it."

"Do you have any idea how much she knows about the past, you know, Mom and Ruth and all of those things?"

"Not really. I mean, she *must* know he had two wives who died. She definitely feels badly for him, like she knows he's been through a lot. I don't know if he ever told her that Mom shot herself or how he fought so much with Ruth."

"So, you've never talked about those things with her?" Carol asked.

"No. I didn't think it was my place to talk about those things, unless she brought it up. Have you?"

"Me neither. She's never asked, and I sure as heck don't want to talk about it. I hate even thinking about it."

On November 12, Carol had a second son. Richard Jr. While the Old Boy became a three-time grandfather, Demi witnessed his mental state deteriorating. His daytime moods began to match the darkness of his night terrors. Whether she realized it or not, her husband was repeating a pattern. When he wasn't on duty, his commitment to drinking escalated beyond her control.

*"But the division in him was a sorrow and a torment, and
he became accustomed to it only as one gets used to an
unhealed and frequently reopened wound."*
~Boris Pasternak, Doctor Zhivago

1951. Demi unwittingly struck an earthshaking nerve. She had read an article in *Life Magazine* about advancements in psychiatry since World War II, when hundreds of non-psychiatric doctors were forced to deal with a wide range of psychiatric issues arising from men coping with life and death situations during and after combat. Featured in the article were excerpts from Albert Deutsch's 1948 book, the *Shame of the States*, an expose on the cruel conditions in overcrowded state hospitals.

"Carroll, you should read this article. They talk about shell shock from war. Now, they call it Combat Stress Fatigue. Some of the symptoms are nightmares, like yours. I really think you should consider seeing a psychiatrist about it. Maybe they can . . ."

"I don't need a goddamn shrink," he roared back.

"Now, Carroll, don't be so dismissive. Whatever your dreams are about, it's eating away at you. Why not try to get some help for it?"

"What the hell are you saying? I'm not a mental case, God dammit."

"Of course not, but you should know, this talks about how bad things are in mental institutions. It makes me more worried about Joan. I know you don't like to think about it, but I do."

"To hell with *Life Magazine!*" He fired the periodical against the wall and stomped off. With a slam of their apartment door, he retreated to Sparky's Bar. In the week that followed, audible domestic unrest could be heard from the chief's apartment, leading to an unscheduled visit to the Jefferson police station by Mayor Rindfleisch.

"Carroll, we need to talk," the mayor said as he approached his chief seated at his desk.

"Have a seat, Ed," Butch said while gesturing to the chair at the side of his desk.

"I'd rather stand, Carroll," the mayor replied. "I talked to you two months ago about citizens, me included, who have noticed your drinking problems. Last night was the last straw."

Butch appeared to remain stoic. He knew exactly what his boss was talking about.

"When you left Sparky's last night, I got some calls. People thought you were beating your wife. It's not the first time it's happened, either. Jefferson can't have a police chief behaving this way. I need you to resign. Write out your resignation letter and bring it to my office by the end of the day. If you don't, you're fired."

Appearing cornered and embarrassed, Butch made a feeble attempt to downplay his actions. "C'mon, Ed. It was April Fool's Day. Things got a little crazy. We were joking in the bar. When I went home, we had an argument. It wasn't that bad."

"It's happened before. The decision's been made, period. Resign today and word of your behavior doesn't leave Jefferson. If you don't resign, I can't guarantee you'll get a helpful recommendation for work elsewhere."

On Wednesday, April 2, the mayor's office issued a brief press release. Police Chief Carroll Beecher resigned. Effective immediately, Herbert West will serve as Acting Chief for the City of Jefferson.

****

Meanwhile, Joan completed her third year of institutionalization. Records stated the following:

> "Adjustment to colony life has been generally good. She attended school and Occupational Therapy classes for several years and made good progress, particularly in occupational therapy. However, she tended to be quite moody at times and was easily upset by other patients and by circumstances of her various job assignments."

Although it's impossible for me to understand what she experienced, who among us hasn't, at times, been moody or upset by others? Documentation from this period also stated:

"Subsequent checkups showed rapid improvement of her congenital syphilis and both blood and spinal tests have proved negative."

Infected since birth, Joan was now syphilis-free. Beginning in 1945, penicillin was successfully used to cure the disease. If penicillin treatment advancements had begun in the previous decade, an altered Beecher prologue may have also advanced, with rewritten destinies for Marie, Butch and their five children. Perhaps, 1951 would find nineteen-year-old Joan still under Marie's wing somewhere in Milwaukee, helping her mother raise the twins as they entered their teenage years.

34.

IRONY

"He had a knack. Whenever he'd step in a bucket of shit, next thing you know, he steps out with a shine on his shoe. He's a stubborn Kraut with the luck of the Irish. Just like me." ~ Tommy Boy

The next afternoon, Butch reassumed his version of the *lotus position* – parked on his favorite bar stool. He looked Sparky's way. "Have you heard?"

"Hey, Butch. Have I heard? Heard what?"

"I got canned. I'm not your police chief anymore. People complained. Were you one of them? Did you rat me out?"

"Oh man, sorry to hear. Me? Rat you out? That's ridiculous. Hell, if I did that sort of thing I'd be out of business."

"I know, I know. I'm just giving you some shit. Give me the usual."

"Sure thing." While Sparky tapped a Pabst and poured a shot, he asked "So, what are you going to do now, Butch?"

"I don't know. The wife's not talking to me. I guess it's just you and me for the time being," Butch cracked. "If I drink enough, I'm sure I'll think of something."

Into his second week of thinking at Sparky's, the mayor walked in to sit next to his former chief. "Carroll, I've got a lead on some work for you, if you're interested."

"No shit, Ed. Tell me about it while I buy you a drink."

Ed sat on the stool next to Butch as Sparky grabbed a glass and reached for the PBR tap. "Nope," said Ed, with a one-hand halt gesture. "Thanks, fellas, but I'm here on official business." He turned his attention to Butch. "Are you familiar with the Wisconsin School for Boys in Waukesha?"

"I've heard of it. It's where the bad apples get sent."

"That's one way of putting it," the mayor chuckled. "They're always looking for supervisors with military or a law enforcement background. If you want to look into it, I'll give you a good recommendation."

"Huh. Well, thanks Ed. I just might do that, after I finish getting my load on," Butch said with a jigger of appreciation and a dash of sarcasm.

"Here, I brought this for you." The mayor slid a business-sized envelope he carried in with him next to Butch's beer and shot glasses. "There's a lot of information in there that I had on file about the place. Feel free to read through the file and drop it off back at my office, whenever."

"I will, Ed. Thanks. I appreciate it."

"I think you could do some good there, I really do. I always liked you, Carroll. I know you've had a rough go, but you're a good egg. Like I said, give my name as a reference. I'll help you get in there."

They pressed flesh. Ed left to pursue further burgomaster affairs. Butch ordered another beer. He shook out the envelope's contents and perused it, page by page. Given Butch's plight, Sparky left him

alone to concentrate. Part of the information he read about the
state-funded facility was a nearly one-hundred-year-old historical
summary about the Wisconsin Industrial School for Boys:

"Those committed to its charge are largely unfortunates.
Some of them are born with malformations of mental faculties,
with vicious tempers and low, brutal tendencies. These are the
most unfortunate class with which the school has to deal. They
are not responsible for their vicious tempers and evil dispositions
any more than for their existence of physical appearance. They
have defects which no reformatory school, be it never so strict or
liberal, kind or harsh in its course of training, can wipe out, or
completely bring into subjugation. None of them, however, leave
the institution in as deplorable a condition as that in which they
entered, and many of them are so thoroughly taught in the art of
self-government that they become the best of citizens; but others,
returning with their unfortunate natural viciousness to their old
haunts, overcome and forget all the influence of the Industrial
school, and rapidly fall to ruin or cells in the State Prison. Some
are the victims of unfortunate marriages, quarreling, drinking,
thieving, slothful parents; others are merely bright, intelligent
boys with an extra amount of spirit and mischievousness, and
others are wandering orphans who come within the scope of the
law governing the commitment of children to the institution. Of
all, such a good account can be given. They rapidly yield to the
beneficial influences brought to bear in the schools, workshop and
chapel, and become, in a reasonably short time, good boys, and
ultimately the very best of citizens. In fact, the good, dispositioned
(sic) boys of intelligence sent out from the Industrial School are,
as a general thing, much better prepared to cope single-handed
with the affairs of the world, than those of equal ability who have
not received such training."

Four years after pursing a timely lead from Tommy Boy, he pursued the advice of Sir Edward of Jefferson. Weeks of formalities later, there Butch went. Just as he had done with Marie twenty-some years earlier, Butch fought his way back into Demi's good graces by getting another "good-guy" job, this time, as a supervisor at Wisconsin's version of Boys Town in Waukesha.

———————

Irony came calling when he answered his phone in early 1953.

"Hi Butch, it's Herb down at the station. I hate to be calling to tell you this, but I've got your boys. They broke into Bud's Sporting Goods through a back window, right after Bud closed the place. I caught them red-handed carrying out fishing rods and two tackle boxes full of stuff."

"God dammit! I'm sorry, Herb. I'll be right over," Butch replied, his anger prompting a concerned look from his wife.

"What's wrong?" Demi asked with alarm.

"The boys broke into the sporting goods store and stole some things. I'm going to the station to sort things out and then I'm going to break their necks."

"Oh, my. Please, Butch, don't be too angry," pleaded Demi. "We both did stupid things at that age. Punish them, but don't hit them."

He slipped on shoes and was out the door without a response. Upon arriving at his former office, Herb West was going through some files as Beecher boys Jim and John sat casually on two office chairs. Without a word spoken, Butch walked in calmly, approached his sons and suddenly slapped both boys off their chairs to the floor.

"Whoa, whoa, whoa!" Herb exclaimed while rushing over to wrap grab the ex-chief around the shoulders to hold him back. "Take it easy, now, c'mon, take it easy!"

"They deserve to be in a cell, goddammit!"

"I had them in there, Butch. After I called you, I brought them out when I knew you were coming."

The boys were back on their feet, standing wide-eyed while Herb got between them and their father, hoping to prevent further spontaneous justice. "C'mon, man, calm down, okay? You know the drill. Settle down. Let's sit down so you can sign the release paperwork."

Reluctantly, Butch complied, at least while the current chief was present.

"You know, I'm just surprised, after the last incident," Herb remarked.

"Last incident? What are you talking about?"

Herb's face said, uh-oh. His mouth said, "Oh, aaaa, didn't your wife tell you?"

"Tell me what?"

"They, aaaa, they stole some booze from the beer depot on Racine Street two weeks ago. I went to your apartment and talked to your wife. She gave me money as restitution. I gave the boys a stern warning. They seemed contrite. I figured they learned their lesson and left the punishment to you and your wife."

"Jesus Christ! Well, thanks for that, but obviously they didn't learn their lesson because I never knew about it." Butch paused a few seconds to hold back from berating Herb for leniency. "I'll tell you what. Lock their asses in a cell for the night, would you please?" Butch stood up; teeth clenched. He turned to deliver a parting message to his fourteen-year-old sons. "I'll be back tomorrow to haul your asses to the Boy's Home in Waukesha where you belong." His sons would spend the night in a jail cell, wondering whether or not he meant what he said. Once back home, Demi faced his wrath for keeping the beer depot caper secret.

For the third time in twelve years, the Old Boy moved his family to escape another build-up of shame and paranoia. They moved to Pewaukee to be closer to his job, cutting the distance between his daughters and grandchildren in half.

Before departing, Butch stopped by the mayor's office to bid a final farewell and thanks. Shortly after his visit, Herb popped in to see the mayor.

"Well, Ed, that's that, I guess. You know, it's a strange thing with that guy."

"What do you mean?"

"So, now he supervises kids at an institution, but he sent his own kid to an institution to be supervised."

"Well, Herb, sometimes we get what we deserve. Sometimes we deserve what we get."

———————

Wearied by the three males in her life, Demi took steps to rekindle her coffee-klatch sessions, hoping to find solace with the young woman she believed would understand most. Marge was game. On a springtime Monday, she drove on her own to meet with Demi when the two had the house to themselves.

"They say, boys will be boys, you know. With the trouble your brothers have been getting into, I thought reminding your father about his younger days would temper his anger, you know, to stop him from overreacting." She paused to shake her head in frustration. "He's too stubborn to admit fallibility. He gets so defensive, even when I'm trying to help."

"I hate to hear that, Demi. I'm so sorry."

"Did your father ever tell you about his shenanigans at your brothers' age?"

"He brought up a few fights he won. Of course, he never mentioned the fights he lost," Marge said, with the cheeky flair her step-mother delighted in and sorely missed.

Demi flashed an amused grin. "Did you know as a boy he did his share of stealing, too?"

"No, he never talked about anything like that, though I don't doubt it."

"Well, the apples haven't fallen far from the tree, moreso with John. I think he gets Jim to go along with the mischief. Jim is passive, more of a follower. That John. He's a smooth talker."

"I know what you mean. He's persuasive and he's got that gleam in his eye, like Dad."

"*Mm-Hmm.* With your brothers in high school now, I'm going to encourage them to think about joining the service when they graduate. I say, it will make men out of them. Build some character."

"Does Dad want them to?"

"I honestly don't know. Jim seems to want to be a policeman like your father. John can be so funny, but he can be quite the smart aleck. There aren't any jobs for smart-alecks."

"Maybe he could be a comedian."

"True, although I got to know a few comedian-types at the Big O years ago in Chicago. The Olympic Theater, that is. Back then, everyone called it the Big O. Let me tell you, it's not an easy life. I'm hoping for something better for John."

"Talker that he is, maybe he'll make a good salesman."

"Time will tell, but I have to be honest with you. I am staying with your father because your brothers need a mother. Pardon my language, but if your father doesn't stop being such a son-of-a-bitch, when the boys finish high school, I will leave him."

"I'm sorry to hear that. I know how he can get sometimes. It's so hard to understand because he can be the life of the party other times. Is there anything I can do to help?"

"Yes. It can't hurt for the boys to get some Big Sister advice, now and then. I do what I can but with all they've been through, they need *you*. I've seen how they respect you. You and Carol are like mothers to them. Don't ever stop. Don't ever give up on them."

Marge was moved by the solemnity of Demi's exhortation, taken by the earnestness in her stepmother's eyes. "I will," she replied with a resolute nod, her welled eyes and pursed lips underscored the intense emotion behind her promise.

Demi nodded, mirroring her stepdaughter's emotion. She lowered her head for a moment and shook it. She looked up into Marge's eyes, then off to the side with a pained grimace. "My God. I've never known a man so tortured."

****

I was born December 26, 1953. The Feast of Saint Stephen on the Catholic calendar, hence, my parent's name choice.

Julie was born ten months later, in October 1954. Her namesake was Julia, her father's mother.

Oh, by the way. In 1954, old Tommy Boy's luck ran out. He was sent off to the Wisconsin State Reformatory in Green Bay on a Class G Felony conviction for running an auto theft ring. He and Butch would never see each other again. Milwaukeeans, at least once upon a time, were fiercely loyal to locally made brands. Most of the cars Tommy stole were made in Wisconsin by Nash. The company went out of business that same year.

Oh, yes. The irony.

35.

TOSS AND TURNS

"And now, for the next 30 minutes: As The World Turns.
*Brought to you today by, Ivory Soap. Ninety-nine and
forty-four one-hundredths percent pure. It floats!"*
~As The World Turns, *soap opera 1956 series premiere, opening theme*

1956. Demi continued to persevere through her two-front
struggle, contending with the highs and lows of raising two
teenage boys and a man bedeviled by sleep disturbances. His night
terrors now had a new twist. On a Saturday morning, when they
had the house to themselves and sensing her man was in a receptive
mood, Demi's resolve elevated to ultimatum.

"Carroll, we can't continue to ignore that. You were talking
and crying in your sleep again last night. After I woke you, you
babbled about smelling tar again. Do you remember?"

"Now that you mention it, yeah. Barely."

"Well guess what? I remember, and not just barely. Your
troubles affect me, too, you know. Your nightmares. I can't get
to sleep after them. It rattles me. It's too disturbing sometimes.
I know you can't help what you do in your sleep, but how many

times have I told you, I think it has to do with how you feel inside about Joan."

He frowned and shook his head.

"Your problems are my problems. This is too important for me to avoid saying anymore. In my heart, I know that Joan being at Southern Colony haunts you. You can't do anything about whatever still weighs on you from the past. Those wives are long gone. I'm here now, and I'm telling you, this is a weight you *can* do something about. How many times have I told you, you need to visit her! You can't just leave her there and forget her. Your conscience won't let you off the hook."

"That's not it," he muttered and paused. "That's not it. It's not that simple."

"Well, then, what is it? I'm your wife. You think I'd put up with all your moods and all your drinking if I didn't love you as much as I do? What is it? Tell me!"

With a far-off look, he could only shake his head again.

"Carroll, I used to dance with feathers, but I can't be an ostrich with my head in the sand anymore. Go see your daughter. The sooner the better."

He still could not reply, though now, he had both arms raised and curled backward across the top of his head, his hands clutching on the back of his head as if he was trying to stop emotional pain from exploding out.

She put her hand on his left shoulder. "I fell in love with you because I saw this beautiful, courageous, strong man who was confident and funny. You need to do something to help me believe I'm still with that man. If you can't, I don't think I can do this anymore."

He lowered his arms slowly, revealing tears trickling down toward his quivering lips. Finally, after a subtle nod, he looked at her. "Okay. I'll go. I'll go see her."

They embraced and cried in each other's arms.

Sometime that April, Butch made the drive from Pewaukee to Union Grove. After meeting with Joan, he met privately with the Southern Colony caseworker assigned to his daughter.

"Thank you for coming, Mr. Beecher. As I touched on a bit over the phone, we regularly evaluate inmates and their potential for moving on to life outside the colony. For those we think are capable, we owe them every opportunity to live their best life. We have to, in order to make room. The flow of incoming men and women never ends."

"So, you're saying she's improved enough to make it out there without causing problems?"

"Yes, we believe she has the potential. In fact, it's quite a coincidence you asked for this meeting. I see our last contact with you was by phone last year, but you were on our list to contact this month. Joan has made maximal use of our educational programs, never presented any serious behavioral problems, and, as you're aware, her physical health has improved significantly."

"Um-hum, still thin but she looks healthy. She was nice enough. A little standoffish, but polite."

"Did she say she wants to leave here?"

"Yes."

"I'm sure you can understand why. We believe she has earned that opportunity. There are few release options to consider. The first is, we release her back into your custody. If that's not a viable option, we can place her on probationary release into one of our foster programs. In one of these programs, we have families who take in young women like Joan on a work placement basis."

Wheels were already turning Joan's way. Her father showed up just in time to share the ride.

June 8, 1956. A Special Clinic Staff Committee granted Joan a temporary discharge to a foster home participating in the work placement program. Protocol during this period meant Joan would live in the exclusive custody of the anonymous family, disallowed to leave unless accompanied.

January 28, 1957. Joan's work program assignment finished with mixed results. She was reassigned to a foster family in Milwaukee; disallowed to leave unaccompanied for 90 days, with potential to reward Joan with expanded privileges outside the home after 90 days.

April 28, 1957. After a satisfactory evaluation of performance and behavior, Joan was granted permission to leave the home with foster participant approval. She was expected to specify where she was planning to go. Her return time had to be mutually agreed upon. For the first time in nearly 15 years, Joan had her first tastes of full independence, one small bite at a time. It was also agreed that the address of her foster family could be revealed to her father and sisters. The stage was finally set for Joan to reunite with her family. Over the next week, a meeting location was agreed upon.

Sunday, May 12, 1957. Joan meets her father and sisters on Mother's Day at McGovern Park on Milwaukee's far north side. A total of 3,311 days had passed since Joan's departure from the Beecher's home in Jefferson.

*L-to-R: Richard Sierlecki Jr., Joan, Victor Sierlecki, Marge with
daughter Julie, Carroll "Butch" Beecher, Carol Sierlecki,
Daniel Kortmann with his father, Wilbur "Korty" Kortmann.
(Kortmann family photo – May 1957)*

*"While there is perhaps a province in which the photograph can tell
us nothing more than what we see with our own eyes, there is another
in which it proves to us how little our eyes permit us to see."*
~Dorothea Lange

L-to-R: The Beecher Sisters – Joan, Marge, and Carol.
(Kortmann family photo – May 1957)

****

Two are missing from the group photo of nine: me and my father, who took the picture. Maybe I was clinging to his pant leg. After years of isolation, Joan appears genuinely happy to see and touch her nephews for the first time. Understandably, she stood for both pictures next to Marge, the sister who corresponded with her the most during their years apart. I deduced that my mother was three months pregnant then. Could she have shared the news for the first time that day?

36.

DELIVERANCE

Back in Pewaukee, Butch and Demi's nest had emptied. By the time the twins reached late adolescence, both were chips off the old block, in terms of quick-wit and teen heartthrob looks. Their struggle to finish high school echoed the ordeal of living with their father. The brightest light in their daily lives was Demi. Decades later, she reflected on those days and how she viewed her stepsons as they began lives of their own.

"I hate to say it, but their father's browbeating shrank their self-confidence. Those poor boys, so much instability, not having a real mother for almost all of their first ten years. On top of that, their father was so hard on them. Jim was the more docile of the two. Strait-laced. Child-like innocence. So handsome. He had that smoky-eyed look like Elvis. Girls were crazy about him, but he was indifferent about all the female attention. It made me wonder about his sexuality. I could tell, he really wanted to be like his dad. He couldn't wait to enlist in the Air Force, really wanted to prove himself. It made his father happy. I was all for it, too.

"John was just the opposite. He returned affection with affection moreso than Jim. He'd work on his hair, all slicked back, that greaser look, you know?" Demi laughed. "He liked looking the tough guy look, but he smiled a lot, and such a great smile.

Girls were crazy about him. He knew it, and he loved it. Many times, I told him to watch his Ps and Qs. Even had a *just between you and me* talk to warn him about casual sex and the truth behind what caused his sister's birth defects. He got the message alright, but after that, he would butt heads with his dad more than ever. So many harsh words back and forth. A few times, I worried it would come to blows. Thank God, it never did. He couldn't wait to move out. Never seemed concerned about how he'd make his way. He got a job right away with Jaeger Baking Company. It's funny, he didn't want to be like his dad, but there he was, driving a delivery route, just like his father did at age twenty, except legally. The one that was less like his father wanted to be like him. The one more like his father didn't want to be. I don't think they had room inside to think much about Joan. They learned to be wary of attachment. They both had their own Oedipus thing to contend with."

That summer, Butch resigned his post at the Wisconsin School for Boys. He took a job at the Miller Brewing Company main plant on State Street, where he would work as a security officer. He circled back to Milwaukee, where he and Demi moved into an apartment building just a few blocks east of the brewery, at 3620 West Kilbourn Avenue.

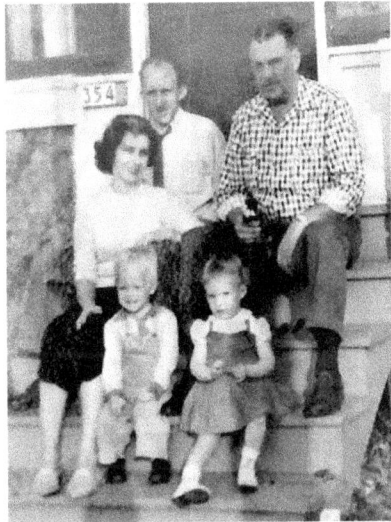

Grandpa (top-right), me and Julie (bottom) at her parents' home on Julia Street. (Kortmann family photo c. 1957)

September 5, 1957. Demi answered the phone on a Friday afternoon.

"Yes, hello, my name is Doris (not her actual name). I'm a caseworker with the Milwaukee Catholic Social Welfare Bureau (CSWB). Could I speak with Mr. Beecher, please?"

"He's at work, but I'm his wife. Can I help you with something?"

"Oh, I'm sorry, our records indicate that Mr. Beecher is a widower."

"He was," Demi replied with a chuckle. "I'm his wife now. Have been for almost nine years. I'm sure of it."

"I'm sorry, Mrs. Beecher. My apologies. The reason for my call is to discuss a matter regarding Joan Beecher, Mr. Beecher's daughter. May I discuss it with you, or would it be best to speak with Mr. Beecher directly?"

"Yes, you should talk with him."

Demi jotted Doris's telephone number. Butch returned her call the next day.

"Oh, hello, Mr. Beecher and thanks for returning my call. I take it you've heard your daughter's caseworker responsibilities have been transferred over to me."

"No, I have not. Why would that be?"

"Ah. Well, my apologies, sometimes changes like these are not as orderly as we'd like them to be. Developments with your daughter prompted the change. There is no reason for alarm. Joan is doing fine, however, my reason for calling you yesterday was to inform you she is pregnant."

"Pregnant! How in the hell could she be pregnant?"

"Apparently, during her recess hours away from her foster home in the last few months, she reconnected with a man from her past, a former Southern Colony inmate."

"Oh, for Christ's sake. Are you sure she's pregnant?"

"Yes. I meet with her biweekly. When we met two weeks ago, she admitted she was happy that she had not menstruated for two months. She understood that meant she was pregnant. At first, I was skeptical, because she tends to go back and forth with what she tells me sometimes. I had her see a doctor that works with us regularly. He said she initially denied having intercourse, fearing she was in trouble, but she admitted it, eventually. The doctor just confirmed she is 15 weeks along. He projects February 27 as a due date."

Butch said nothing.

"Are you still there, sir?"

"Ja," he affirmed in German. "I guess when the state lets these guys out, they can't make 'em take salt peter anymore."

"That's true, unfortunately."

"So, now what?"

"Well, right now, I'm just calling to notify you. There will be a number of considerations. I'm in the process of gathering information on the alleged father. This hasn't happened often, but when it has, the baby is usually placed into foster care until a suitable family is found to adopt him or her. What are your initial thoughts on Joan keeping the baby or the potential for someone in the Beecher relation to adopt?"

"No and no. How's that?"

"Alright, well, can I assume you would still like me to keep you in the loop as things progress?"

"Absolutely, and I'm sorry, I didn't mean that. I'll go along with whatever plans are made for her to get through this."

———————

Over the next several weeks, the news filtered back to Joan's sisters. Details about the alleged father also made their way back to Butch through caseworker, Doris. He wanted to know more about the man who inseminated his daughter:

"*The alleged father, born in 1930, the oldest of two male siblings. Admitted to Southern Wisconsin Colony on June 26, 1946. Commitment by the County Court of Kenosha County, precipitated by the fact he had become a behavior problem in the home and the community. Initial classification listed post-encephalitis as the causative factor of deficiency. Operating as a high-grade defective demonstrating arrested intelligence. Father born 1886 of Irish descent, died in 1950. Mother born 1900 of German descent. She petitioned the Kenosha County Court in 1952 for a re-examination hearing. Alleged father discharged from Southern Colony April 28, 1952. Now living with his mother and stepfather in Milwaukee.*"

Within the combined caseworker documentation I obtained, Doris's initial assessment of her new client read, in part:

"*The father is at a loss for suggestions on Joan's current situation but will go along with any plans that are made for her. (He) had not seen Joan, except occasionally while at the colony, despite the letters Joan would write to him, asking him to visit. Joan's sisters are married. One has advised her to secure an abortion. Joan was sent to St. Coletta's daily from home but attended only a few months when that institution advised her removal to Southern Colony, where she has lived since then, until February of this year. Miss (Joan's caseworker at the colony) described Joan as being submissive to authority, as presented in the colony, more so recently, because on this depends her release, which she desires very much. My predecessor states Joan is inclined to be evasive and untruthful, if she thinks telling the truth will make things difficult for her. For example, after readily acknowledging her pregnancy symptoms and the possibility of being pregnant, she became alarmed and denied having vomited or having had relations. She is somewhat naïve and is reserved with strangers.*"

September 23. After Doris identified a family willing to take in a work placement candidate the previous week, Joan spent her first night in their home. It was the night of the *Shot Heard 'Round Wisconsin*, when the Braves Henry Aaron smacked an 11th inning home run to propel Milwaukee into the World Series for the first time ever. One week later, the mother from Joan's work placement home called to report difficulty with Joan. Doris documented the details:

> *"(She) did a very good job at housekeeping but is unable to take on the job of caring for the children. She gets along so well with the children, who are terribly fond of her, mainly because she is more like a playmate because she is so near their age, mentally. The mother said an incident her eight-year-old told her about scared the life out of her. Joan had the children out for a walk. As she began to lead them across the street, a car turned down the block and headed in their direction. Joan panicked and ran off, leaving the children behind in the middle of the street. The mother complained that Joan had broken a few things, including some items of value from a collection of her husbands. Joan cried and said she feels so bad after doing such things. The mother said it is impossible for her to yell at Joan but said it's been terribly hard on her patience."*

October 16. The foster mother had persevered with Joan for two more weeks. During that time, Doris completed arrangements for Joan to enter a CSWB maternity program for unwed mothers earlier than planned. On this day, Joan left the foster home to live in the care of nuns at a Catholic maternity home in Milwaukee for the duration of her pregnancy. Though Joan was still on temporary discharge status from Southern Colony, the CSWB committed to overseeing Joan's ordeal and the fate of her baby. A week later, Doris had her first meeting with the alleged father. He shared that he just started a new job and that he and Joan very much wanted to keep the baby and marry before the child was born.

November 1957 to February 1958. Carol had her fourth child and first daughter. She was named Mary. Joan experienced a variety of ups and downs in the months leading up to her due date, as described in the following caseworker documentation excerpts:

"Joan said that she and the alleged father decided they would release the baby for adoption. I explained to Joan that the alleged father had been in to see me and that the two of you desperately wanted to get married. Joan said it should be alright for them to marry and that there was nothing anyone could do to stop it. She said if anyone tried, they would certainly continue their relationship and there would probably be more illegitimate children. I agreed that releasing the baby as a good decision, as they would be able to make more of a go of their marriage because it would be difficult financially to start out with a child without any money. Joan is frustrated over not having received any money from her father. She feels badly her father apparently has not responded to her efforts to contact him. She realizes he had never paid much attention to her at Southern Colony and that she has never been able to face the reality that her father really did not care for her at all. She shared that the alleged father's mother went into a rage when they told her they were giving up rights to the child. Joan was upset she had not received any birthday cards for her 25th birthday, not even from the alleged father. Joan said she had a nice holiday season and spent Christmas Day with Marge and her family. Her father had sent a cab for her on New Year's Day. She was quite pleased at this and now that she had seen her family, she was thinking about keeping the baby after all. We spoke about this further during the interview and I noticed she was changing her mind back and forth over keeping

the baby or giving it up. I feel she will be undecided the rest of the pregnancy and it would be difficult for her to maintain a decision until the end. Joan changes her mind as quickly as she changes her moods. She said her father gave her five dollars on New Year's and told her he would like her to see him again sometime and that any time she would like to come, he would send a cab for her. I wondered how much of this is real or if a lot of it is in her fantasies, as she has never been able to admit to herself that her father is not very attentive of her. She is fearful of admitting to herself that he is somewhat rejecting of her. In my last few interviews, she hops from one topic to another, as usual. The nun caring for her had also noticed this and that she is becoming a great deal more emotional as of late. She talks about her family a great deal and how interested they are in her; however, they have expressed no interest whatsoever, nor do they call up or write to her. She still feels as though she will give the child up."

Friday February 28, 1958. Joan gives birth to Baby Margaret.

Monday March 3. Doris phones Butch to report the girl's birth on Friday and that mother and baby were doing well. Demi offers to relay the news to Marge and Carol. After doing so, Marge calls Carol that night.

"We should go see Joan and the baby, don't you think?" Marge asks.

"I suppose. Then again, I don't know. I'm really not comfortable seeing the baby. I'm not sure I feel right about going right now. I'm worried she will expect one of us to adopt the baby at the last minute."

"You know, now that you say that, I think you're right. It probably is better to wait."

Friday March 7. Baby Margaret is placed into a foster home through the CSWB. Joan is moved from the maternity home to a Catholic Halfway House to live for an unspecified amount of time until she can find a place to live.

Saturday March 22. Marge picks up Carol and drives to the maternity home. A nun guides them to Joan's room.

"I must look huge, huh?" Joan quips while she exchanges hugs with her sisters.

"You look great, Joan. You haven't put on nearly as much baby weight as I have," reassures Carol. "You look way better than me, and it's been almost four months since I had Mary. It's getting harder and harder to get rid of it."

"Carol's right, Joanie. So how are you feeling?"

"Terrible. My body feels okay, but I feel terrible."

Her sisters could not find the words to reply. They nodded. Carol clutched one of Joan's hands. Marge stroked Joan's hair back from her forehead and repeated her stroke gently a few more times.

Joan began to cry. "I've had such an awful life. So many things, bad things, that, that have, happened to me, that made me cry, and cry." Her words came haltingly, from one word to the other, mixed with crying and breathing. "Now this. I've never, I never cried, like this. Never. I've cried so much. I had to, had to let, go, of, Baby Margaret."

Carol and Marge slid their chairs to flank Joan on each side. Both struggled to hold back tears of their own, caressing their sister with soothing strokes of physical consolation as she sobbed uncontrollably for over a minute.

"I didn't even cry this much when Mama died. I've been thinking of Mama. How she felt. What made her so sad that she could never have Danny. So now. Now I know how she felt. Now I know."

Weeping. The sound of three women weeping.

"Is everything going to be okay here?" asked a nun who passed by their door.

With wet eyes, Marge smiled through her grimace and waved off the concerned nun. Moments later, the nun returned and handed a box of tissues to Carol.

Carol pulled out several tissues. "Here you go, hon," she said while handing them to Joan. "I'm so sorry for you."

"Me too, sweetie, me too," Marge echoed.

A few more minutes passed before Joan regained her composure. Finally, she sat back into her chair and declared, "I'm okay now."

"Well, that's good because we're running out of tissues," Marge quipped. Her gift for quick-witted one-liners was timed perfectly. They united in purifying laughter, reminiscent of the many times they had helped each other through so many painful moments the previous decade.

"You know, having a baby was the greatest thing I've ever done," said Joan with proud certainty. "And then, having Baby Margaret come out of me and go away forever is the hardest thing I ever had to do."

"I'm sure," Carol said. She placed her left hand onto Joan's right hand and nodded solemnly to acknowledge the magnitude of what her sister had accomplished.

"We're so proud of you, Joan," said Marge. She extended her right arm across Joan's shoulders and playfully added in her best Doris Day singing voice:

> *"We love you,*
> *a bushel and a peck,*
> *and a hug around the neck,*
> *a hug around the neck."*

———————

Marge and Joan's Aunt Minette held discussions with Doris about adopting Baby Margaret. Ultimately, all parties agreed that releasing the child to an anonymous CSWB-approved family was the best option, avoiding the likelihood of boundary issues arising when the child's home was known to the birth mother.

At seven months old, Joan's baby girl was adopted by a Sheboygan family.

April 1959. Joan marries the baby's father, James "Jimmy" Ward.

June 22, 1959. Carol delivers her fifth child. My new brother is named Philip.

37.

SIXTIES AND SUN

"Like an old dusty road
I get weary from the load
Movin' on, movin' on
Like this tired troubled earth
I've been rollin' since my birth
Movin' on, movin' on

There's a place in the sun
Where there's hope for ev'ryone
Where my poor restless heart's gotta run
There's a place in the sun
And before my life is done
Got to find me a place in the sun,"
~Stevie Wonder (1966)

1960. I finished first grade. That summer, my parents moved to the four-bedroom house on Melvina Street where they would live out the rest of their lives. With the birth of my younger sisters, Monica in 1961 and Laura in 1964, their brood topped out at seven. They enrolled me and my older brothers at Saint Margaret Mary Grade School, where I was made to repeat First Grade. Apparently, I needed to be cleansed of my heathen year of programming from John Muir Public Elementary. My mother won the unofficial title for most prolific Beecher Sister babymaker.

Beecher Sister Number Two, Marge, had a third child, Jill, born in 1963. Marge and husband Korty had moved to a new subdivision in a farm country setting in 1958. Set on a one-acre lot, their home would become the focal point for Beecher family gatherings for decades to come.

Beecher Sister Number Three never wandered again. Joan finally had what she had always craved, freedom and unconditional love. She found a soulmate in Jimmy. They made a home for themselves on North 46th Street in the city's Parklawn Housing Project. Determined to have a family of their own, they had two daughters, Mary, born in 1960 and Kathy, born in 1962. Later, they had a son, Jimmy Jr., born in 1968. All three were intellectually and physically normal.

Demi feathered her apartment nest by lavishing Butch with exceptional cooking, garnished with sage advice: "Enjoy the rest of your life . . . enjoy time with your daughters . . . offer moral support to your sons . . . enjoy time with your grandchildren." Though Butch rarely verbalized his acquiescence, his actions showed it. Years later, Demi said the sixties were their best years together, by far.

"When he wasn't working at Miller, he never went anywhere without me. If we stopped at a tavern for a drink or a fish fry, when I would say it's time to go, we left. Without a doubt, our favorite thing to do was visiting his daughters and all the grandkids. Nothing, and I mean nothing ever came close to making him as happy as when he was around those kids. He got such a kick out of bringing them treats. Even if he was in a blue mood, once we started driving to a daughter's house, he'd turn happy, getting into character to play his favorite role – Grandpa Beecher."

According to Demi, the Old Boy achieved two personal breakthroughs in aspects of modern living he was embarrassed to admit. She helped him confront a fear of flying and an almost equal fear of driving on the city's freeway system once it opened in 1958.

"In '62, I coaxed him into a vacation trip to Mexico by airplane. I didn't dare tell anyone how nervous he got. I mean, I had never flown before either, but I was excited to finally find out what it was like. Him? His face got so pale, I thought he would faint. When the plane took off, his hands were shaking and his knuckles turned so white, I thought he might bend the seat arms," she recalled with a chuckle. "Once we got to cruising altitude and he downed a Brandy Manhattan or two, he turned into a pussy cat. By the time we were landing, he was so tipsy, I don't think he even knew it was happening. We both had a good laugh about it over coffee the next morning. When we ate, I liked trying out local dishes. Not your Grandpa. He'd order American food, always asked for Miller beer. He wanted nothing to do with Mexican beers. You can take the boy out of Milwaukee, but you can't take Milwaukee out of the boy. We brought back two shopping bags filled with Mexican souvenirs for the grandkids. Once we got back, he couldn't wait to make plans for making the rounds and hand out the toys and hats like Santa.

"He drove on the freeway system only a few times and only as a last resort. When he did, he wouldn't budge from the right lane with the slower traffic. I pretended not to notice how skittish he'd get. Richard and Korty would tease him about it. I couldn't. After all, a lot of people our age had trouble with driving so close to so many fast-moving cars all at once. I was proud of him, though I admit I thought it was strange for a man, so bold in other many ways, to fear what most men *and women* seemed to take in stride.

"All I ever wanted is for him to relax and enjoy himself. Helping him do that was sometimes more than I could take. I needed an outlet, a break from sharing the weight he carried. That's really why I took that part-time job at Herring's Restaurant on 35th Street. Sometimes I'd cook, sometimes I'd waitress. We both had our little jobs to go off to. It made our time together better. We never talked about the past anymore. Neither did your mother, or her sisters and brothers. It was too dark there. Better to embrace the sun than inherit the wind."

*L-to-R: Me in my Milwaukee Braves shirt, Victor, Phil,
Grandpa Beecher on his birthday, Daniel, Julie, Mary and
Dick (Richard Jr.) holding his souvenir cap from Mexico.
(c. 1962 – photo credit unknown)*

38.

DEAR OPA

May 5, 1964. Carol received an unexpected phone call. On the line was a beloved voice from the past that she hadn't heard in years. She recognized it immediately.

"Hi, Carol, this is your Aunt Dorothy."

"Oh, my goodness, Aunt Dot! How are you?"

"I'm doing just fine, sweetheart. How are you?"

"Oh, good, good. I have my hands full, just had a baby last month. A girl. We named her Laura."

"Oh, my! Congratulations! How many does that make for you now?"

"Seven," replied Carol with a laugh. "Never a dull moment here. What's going on with you and yours out in California?"

"Your Uncle Jerry and I are well. Marty, my youngest, moved out last year. We're empty nesters now."

"It's crazy, how fast the time goes, isn't it? Your nest is empty and mine is about as full as it can get."

"Look, Carol, we just flew into Milwaukee. Your grandfather's health is failing. I don't know how much time he has left but I came back to be with him while I still can. Agnes and I wanted you to know."

"Oh, God, no, I'm so sorry, I didn't know. I haven't seen him for a few years, but I talk with Agnes on the phone every so often. She usually lets me know how he's doing."

"I know, she just told me the last time the two of you talked was around Christmas. John's been in and out of the hospital the last few months. Agnes has been so busy taking care of him lately. Now that I'm here, she asked me to get in touch with the Beecher girls, so I called you first. I was going to call Marge next and Joanie, too, if you can tell me how I can reach her."

"Of course. We were thinking of getting together on Mother's Day. What if we were to go see him next Sunday?"

"That would be wonderful! He's still at home for now. I don't know how much longer he can stay there. The way things are going, he may need to go into nursing care somewhere soon."

"Well, I'm so glad you called. How long are you in town? Will we be able to see you when we visit Grandpa John?"

"You sure will. I'm not sure how long Jerry and I are going to stay, but we'll definitely still be here next weekend. I can't wait to see you all, especially on Mother's Day!"

———————

Sunday, May 12.

Marge drove off in her nine-passenger Ford station wagon with son Daniel and daughters Julie and Jill. She stopped at Joan's house to pick her up and then went to pick up Carol, accompanied by her three oldest sons, including me. Apparently, my mother and aunt wanted their Grandpa John to see as many of his great-grandchildren as possible, for what might be the last time. We arrived at John's house on 21ˢᵗ Street, his home since the 1920s. Mom's aunts, Agnes and Dorothy, welcomed us in. They led the nine of us to John's bedroom. My God, the man was eighty-eight. I had never been so close up to someone that old before. He said some things to Ma and my aunts. His voice was weak. He thanked each of his three granddaughters individually, with halting words of affection.

"Thank you for all you did for us. I love you," Ma said to him. She had tears in her eyes.

Aunt Marge reached to clutch his hand. "Love you, Opa. Thank you for everything. We will never forget you."

"Thank you," Aunt Joan said. "I remember you always had me sit by you. You always made me feel better. You and Aunt Dot and Aunt Agnes."

As Joan spoke, I saw that Mom and Aunt Marge fought to hold back their tears. Ma turned away, trying to hide her emotion from us.

When Joan receded, Marge gathered the children along his bedside. "Six of your great-grandchildren are here to see you, Opa. They've grown so fast. Daniel and Victor will start driving next year." We stood awkwardly, unsure of how to react or what to say.

"My sweet children," John began. "I know it must be frightening to see such a sick old man. I was born in 1875. I can't really see faces anymore but I can tell you are there." He stopped for a few seconds to catch his breath. "I knew your mothers when they were your age. Your mothers lived through some very hard times back then. They are brave. They are strong. Never stop. Never stop loving them with all your heart.

Stopping again, this time he turned toward the nightstand, reaching slowly for his water glass. Joan stood adjacent to the stand. Seeing him struggle to grasp the glass, she picked it up, guiding it into his hand and held it with him until he had control of it. Nearly a full minute passed while he took three deliberate sips. When he was finished, Joan helped him set the glass back down. He paused for about ten more seconds, as if scanning his memory and gathered the strength to manage a few more words.

"I used to write music and poems." He paused once more. "I have one for you. It goes like this:

> *Mothers are the strongest branches in every family tree*
> *All their love and sacrifice, you never truly see*
> *They live inside your heart and there they will always be.*

"Please. Remember that for me, won't you?"

I nodded, along with the other five. At the time, none of us could understand the depth of his meaning, unaware of the profound history behind the words.

Our time in John's bedroom was over in less than twenty minutes. Agnes and Dorothy thanked us for coming and walked out with us to the street to say goodbye.

Aunt Marge began driving away with Aunt Joan next to her and Mom on the right side of the front seat holding little Jill. Daniel, Victor and Dick filled the station wagon's middle bench seat. Me and Julie got to sit in those keen seats in the way-back where kids could sit face-to-face.

Ma turned to her left to look back at us. "I'm proud of all of you. You were well behaved. I'm sure it meant a lot to him that you came."

"They sure were. I'm glad you came, too. I'm glad *I* came," echoed Joan.

Marge chimed in. "Someday, we will tell you more about your great-grandfather and the things we lived through with him a long time ago."

"He was known for playing the pipe organ at Gesu Church for a long time, right?" said Victor.

"We're all here. What else is there to know?" wondered Daniel.

His mother replied "Now is not the time. Trust me. Someday, my boy. Someday."

Mom and Aunt Joan still had sniffles and were wiping their
eyes. Silence filled the Ford. Even us kids knew. It was time to shut
up and ride.

John Baptist Leicht died June 7, 1964.

John Leicht – c. 1932
(Photo via Martin Weirich genealogical archive)

39.

THE PARTY'S OVER

When it came to family fun, in fact, any kind of fun, it was Marge's world. Everyone wanted to be in it. Carol was the eldest daughter, but she wasn't cut out for the role of matriarch. She never saw herself in that role. Neither did Marge, really. Her emergence as unofficial family leader happened organically. Carol had a heart of gold but had been cautious all her life about who she shared it with. Marge had a golden heart with infinite capacity. Since 1958, her house was *the* place to be for housewives and kids in the Pollber Heights Subdivision. Within the family, her commitment to helping her brothers make their way was saintly. She took John in when he was down on his luck, introducing him to Diane, a neighborhood woman. They wound up married. When brother Jim's time in the Air Force ended, Marge took him in until he found a job and could support himself.

––––––––

Sunday, February 13, 1966. For the second year in a row, Marge threw a Valentine's Day party. She had done it the previous year for some mid-winter fun to stave off cabin-fever. Everyone loved it, none moreso than her father.

"I never saw him happier," she said afterward. "Demi said the Old Boy took home all the Valentine's cards from the grandkids. He hung them up in every room of their apartment."

Party arrival time was 1:30 to 2:00 p.m., which afforded guests time to attend Mass in the morning, something Marge no longer did. Hubby, Korty, was raised Lutheran. His longstanding distaste for Catholic rules and aggressive donation tactics reached a breaking point in 1965. He was done carrying a cross, Catholic or otherwise. Free-spirited Marge needed no coaxing to see it his way. Their newfound, Sunday freedom gave them more time to enjoy life on their terms, giving Marge more time for things like Valentine parties.

By two o'clock, everyone had arrived except Butch and Demi. That would not be cause for alarm for most people. It *was* with Butch, a world-class stickler for punctuality. At 2:15 p.m., Marge called their apartment but didn't get an answer. Ten minutes later, she was relieved to see him pull into the driveway. His Mercury had no damage, so he hadn't been in a wreck, but when he ambled in with Demi, it was plain to see. *He* was the wreck. The last time everyone had seen him was Christmas Day. He'd appeared to be fine. Forty days later, he was ashen, gaunt and listless. His greeting was a wave and a forced smile.

"Sorry we're late. Grandpa isn't feeling too good today," Demi greeted. "I was about to call to let you know we weren't going to come but your dad insisted."

"Good lord, Dad, you look terrible!" Marge said with alarm.

"I've been a little under the weather, but I had to come," he replied.

Demi added, "He wanted all the kids to get Valentines he made."

"Have you seen a doctor?" Carol asked.

"No," Demi answered for him. "You know your father, stubborn as they come."

Butch gave Demi *the look*, though he said nothing to refute her.

"Here, have a seat," Korty said, pushing the chair he was in toward his father-in-law.

Butch sat, paper bag of Valentines in hand. Fighting off denial, Marge brought him his traditional set-up: a shot, a glass of beer and an egg. He didn't touch it, opting for water at Demi's insistence. Despite the sick elephant in the room, the adults flailed for an hour or two in a pathetic attempt at normalcy for the sake of the children. The party was over. Everyone knew it. Especially the children.

On Monday, Marge called the Visiting Nurses Association. She arranged for a nurse to come to her father's Kilbourn Avenue apartment the next day. When the nurse arrived Tuesday, she buzzed Apartment 3.

"It's Sheila Anderson with the Visiting Nurses Association. I'm here to see Mr. Beecher."

The very second after Demi buzzed her in, Butch grumbled from his recliner. "I'm not seeing a goddamn nurse."

His wife ignored him. She opened their apartment door and greeted Nurse Anderson.

"Thank you for coming. Please come in."

Butch growled once more. "I told you, I'm not seeing a nurse!"

Demi rolled her eyes and exhaled with a *you've-got-to-be-kidding* sigh. "Carroll, that is enough! Marge sent the nurse here, and I'm all for it. You're suffering. I can't stand it anymore! We're trying to help you. Now let her do her job."

"What I got, there ain't no cure for."

"Mr. Beecher, I'm really sorry you haven't been well. When your daughter informed me that you are a retired Milwaukee police officer, I jumped at the chance to help you. My own father was a Chicago policeman, so I know how she feels. You have loved ones who care deeply for you. Please, allow me the honor of giving you a very basic exam. Let's get to the bottom of what's wrong."

He stared out the window for a while. He lowered his head and finally looked over at the nurse. With a tone of resignation, he uttered, "Fine."

Nurse Anderson's emotional appeal succeeded. She conducted a rudimentary exam and advised that a more thorough exam and testing should be done as soon as possible.

Butch had nothing to say.

"If you could help me make arrangements to get that started, I would appreciate it very much," Demi said. On Friday, February 18, Butch checked into Mount Sinai Hospital on North 12th Street. Since Demi did not have a driver's license, Marge made the trip across town to pick up her father and take him in.

After a week had passed, a diagnosis was in. Advanced bronchogenic carcinoma. It had metastasized from his lungs to his liver.

Surgical intervention was no longer viable. Chemotherapy and radioembolization treatments were ruled out. His internal state was beyond the ability to withstand it. The prognosis was exactly as bad as Butch had feared. One to three months. Doctors had administered pain killers and some transfusions during his stay. At the very least, palliative care helped him to feel somewhat better. Demi insisted that he be given the opportunity to live out his days at home. His oncologist released him on March 4 with instructions to get his affairs in order.

Once he was back home, Butch specified some ground rules for Demi to follow.

"Check with me first before you let anyone in or anyone asks to come over. It's bad enough feeling like shit. I don't want anyone to see me this way. Especially the kids."

"Of course, Carroll. You have my word," Demi promised.

"Another thing. I don't want to talk to anyone on the phone. If Marge and Korty or Carol and Dick want to come over, that's fine, but tell them I don't want to talk about being sick. They can tell me about the kids or tell me jokes or whatever but not this shit."

"What about the Wards and your boys?"

"Oh, hell, they don't want to see me."

"Of course, they do."

"We'll see," he replied skeptically.

"By the way, I have to call your boss to give him an update. Is there anyone else from work I should tell?

"Charlie, I guess would be okay."

"He'll want to see you, I'm sure. You two go back a long way." Demi knew how special Charles "Charlie" Becker was. They'd served on the force in District 5 for several years, beginning in 1934 when they worked the Transit Strike together. Charlie was one of three former Milwaukee policemen on staff at Miller Brewing Company. He'd helped Butch get his job at Miller eight years earlier.

During the next two weekends, all five of his children and their four spouses visited the dying Beecher patriarch. Demi remembered how difficult it was.

"It was so hard for him, for everyone, of course. Respecting his wishes to not talk about the cancer or how he was feeling was like walking on eggs. Marge and Dick did most of the talking, things about the kids and so forth, but otherwise it was so surreal. So sad. He just sat in his recliner. It was hardest on Carol. She was fighting the whole time to keep from breaking down. John or Korty would try to say something funny to lighten things up. Carol would laugh and cry at the same time. She was always attached to her father more than anyone else. She adored him. She really did. That last weekend, he was in bed when they came, so no one stayed long. What I remember most was it was the 20th. It was Carol's youngest daughter's birthday. Laura turned two years old. Carol knew he didn't want any of the grandchildren to see him, but it was something she felt he would like. I'm so glad she did. She was right. Carol told her to hold grandpa's hand. Oh, my lord. He smiled, tears trickling down his cheeks. It made me cry. I think everyone did."

40.

LAST CALL

March 25. Demi could no longer care for Butch on her own. An ambulance crew transported him back to Mount Sinai. She was told the end would come in a matter of days, perhaps a week or two. Once back home, she made ten or fifteen phone calls to get the word out.

In the days that followed, several members of the Milwaukee police force, past and present came for short visits to say good-bye. Most notably among them was current Milwaukee Police Chief, Harold Breier, who Butch had helped train when Breier joined the force as a patrolman in 1940.

Charlie Becker, Butch's longtime friend and colleague came to see him with another old friend. It was Helen Cromwell, AKA Dirty Helen. Butch hadn't seen Helen since she was forced to close the legendary Sunflower Inn ten years earlier.

"Hey, Butchie, look who I brought to see you," Charlie said when he entered Butch's hospital room with Helen.

Butch managed a smile. His eyes widened, revealing eye whites that had yellowed. Their coloring less pronounced than the yellowish-orange cast of his skin, jaundiced by liver failure.

Helen being Helen, greeted him with gallows humor. "Butch,

you look like hell." No one laughed. "I tried to smuggle in a bottle of Old Fitz, but the nurses took it away."

Trying his best to return the joke, Butch answered, his voice weak and barely recognizable. "I haven't had a drink or a smoke for a month. It's been hell," he deadpanned.

"We had some good times, didn't we?" Charlie said. "Remember when we got that new shift captain? We drove him nuts for a month," Charlie said, sharing the story just as much for Helen's benefit. "I kept telling the new guy that I was Beecher. This guy would say he was Becker. We drove the guy nuts 'til he threatened to write us up."

Charlie's story tickled Butch's laugh reflex. It caused him to cough, and he winced from the searing pain in his stomach.

"Sorry I made you laugh, my friend," Charlie apologized.

Helen expressed her affection. "Butch, I just want you to know I was always proud to know you. Heck, you were like a son to me. Remember how I would always say, live a little? Well, you sure as hell did. Love ya, my friend."

With tightened lips, he nodded as his welled eyes began to overflow. He struggled mightily, managing to eke out "Love you, too." His words were barely audible, parsed by air puffing through his quivering lips.

Charlie couldn't take it anymore. With tightened lips, he reached out to shake hands one last time. Butch returned a squeezed, not a shake, the finality of the moment written in his eyes.

Helen blew Butch a kiss. She and Charlie turned and disappeared into the hallway.

April 2. It was a Saturday, and Marge decided it would be a visit for the Beecher sisters only. In her Ford station wagon, she picked up

Carol and then Joan, arriving at Mount Sinai just before 11:00 a.m. The Old Boy was sedated and lapsing in and out of consciousness. His daughters stood at his bedside.

"We're here, Dad," said Marge first.

"I'm here, Dad," said Carol next.

"Me, too," Joan said.

The sound of their voices roused his attention. His eyes opened. Gazing at his three daughters, a faint smile came to his face. Two nurses entered, each carrying a folding chair so that all three women could sit at his bedside. For two hours, they made small talk about kids and weather. They also talked about how strange it was for it to be the start of baseball season and the Braves were now in Atlanta, instead of Milwaukee. Their father's eyes would open periodically. Sometimes, he seemed to be listening in as he faded in and out. During their ride to Mount Sinai, Marge supposed that the sound of their voices would give the Old Boy comfort. There was no way of knowing, though periodically his facial expressions seemed to convey hints of pleasure from their presence.

At 1:15 p.m., a nurse entered. "Mr. Beecher? It's Donna. I'm here to give you some more morphine. Have you been drinking some water?"

Carol replied for him. "We gave him some a few times. He sipped a little from the straw."

The nurse's presence seemed to rouse him. He kept his eyes open.

Marge seized the opportunity to try conversing. "Dad. We've been here for a few hours. Did you know you've been singing, *Roll Out the Barrel* in your sleep?"

She hoped a quip would get him to smile. He did.

Carol asked, "Do you feel like talking?"

His mouth opened in slow motion. "It's hard," he answered. The words eked out in a raspy whisper.

"We won't make you talk then," added Marge. "We're going to leave soon, but we'll be back on Monday again. Just the three of us."

Carol and Joan looked at her a bit puzzled. They had yet to discuss visiting the next day, as opposed to Monday, when availability of a sitter for their little ones would be an issue.

Joan asked, "Before we go, could I talk to Dad alone?"

Carol and Marge looked at each other, surprised by their sister's request.

"Sure, sweetie," Marge replied. "We'll be out in the hallway. Come get us when you're done."

After her sisters withdrew, Joan moved a folding chair out of her way in order to stand close to him.

"Dad, I just want you to know that I forgive you. I forgive you for what you did to Mama. I forgive you for sending me away like you did. I talked about it with Jimmy a lot. We decided the best thing is for me to forgive. If you didn't make me live at the colony, I would never have met Jimmy."

He stared back at her. His eyes were wider than they had been all day. He mouthed something. Joan could not make it out. He frowned and shook his head. A tear came down his left cheek, followed by another. He tried to speak again. It caused him to cough to the point of retching. Gasping for air, it took him a full minute to compose himself. His left hand shook as he raised it, palm up, beckoning his daughter to hold his hand. Joan reached out to clutch it. He squeezed her fingers gently. His only means to communicate left. More tears rolled from his eyes. Joan stood tight-lipped. She withdrew her hand. Without saying another word, she walked to the door and opened it.

———————

Monday. April 4. At 4:00 a.m., a nursed made her hourly check in Room 309. She returned to her desk at the nurse's station near the elevators. One by one, she began calling the five phone numbers on the notification list on the chart. Patient Beecher would expire soon.

Before he took his last breath, Demi, the Beecher sisters and their husbands made it to his bedside. Carroll August Beecher died at 5:33 a.m.

Beecher, Policeman Here 14 Years, Dies

Carroll A. Beecher, 60, of 3620 W. Kilbourn av., a Milwaukee policeman for 14 years and former police chief at Jefferson, died Monday of cancer at Mount Sinai hospital, where he had been a patient for two weeks. A native of Milwaukee, Mr. Beecher was a plant guard for the Miller Brewing Co., for the last eight years.

Mr. Beecher

In 1931, he joined the Milwaukee police force and served as a patrolman and acting desk sergeant. Later he was transferred to the bureau of identification.

He left the force in March, 1954, and for a short time operated a tavern. In 1947 he moved to Jefferson and was named police chief there.

Mr. Beecher retired from that post in 1952. He then became a supervisor at the old state school for boys at Waukesha. He left that post 1956 and returned to Milwaukee.

Survivors include his wife Delma; two sons, James and John; three daughters, Mrs Wilbur (Margaret) Kortmann Mrs. James (Joan) Ward and Mrs. Richard (Carol) Sierlecki; and a sister, Mrs. Warner (Minette) Carr, all of Milwaukee.

Funeral service will be at 9 a.m. Wednesday in St. Rose of Lima Catholic church, 3013 W. Michigan st. Burial will be in Calvary cemetery. The body is at the Brett funeral home, 2001 W. Wisconsin av.

Milwaukee Sentinel – *Tuesday, April 5, 1966*
(Chronology errors: 1945 not '54, 1951 not '52, 1957 not '56)

41.

SKELETON DANCE

Seventeen days after their father was buried, the Beecher sisters went to see Demi at her apartment. She invited all of her husband's children to meet privately, without spouses, after they had time to themselves to grieve.

Neither of Demi's stepsons came. Their hearts still smoldered with conflicted feelings. Already on emotional overload, Jim wanted no part of the intimacy anticipated at Demi's postmortem. John's feelings always ran hotter. Being elsewhere was his better part of valor.

The four women gathered at noon. Always a tasteful hostess, Demi spent her morning creating a colorful variety of finger sandwiches, deviled eggs and fruit petit fours.

"Oh, my goodness, Tizzy lish! What a spread," Carol exclaimed in her inimitable way over the gourmet display on Demi's kitchenette table.

"Help yourself, ladies. There is coffee, juice, tea or lemon water on the counter behind you."

With small plates and cloth napkins in hand, they settled into upholstered furnishings in the apartment's small but formal living room.

"Thank you all so much for coming," Demi began. "I know

you've been spending so much time away from your children to be with your father over the past month. I wanted to treat you girls in a special way today while I fill you in on what your dad left to you. He wanted you and the boys to split the funds he saved in a trust account that he set aside just for his children. It comes out to about four thousand dollars for each of you. As you know, he wasn't big on possessions. He willed *The Merc* to Jim. He divided up his personal effects, things like watches, jewelry and police mementos to give to your brothers, also. There is list of other things that he asked me to divide among you three. For example, his prized Grundig-Majestic radio. Carol, your boys were always so fascinated with it, but I would rather have you three decide between yourselves. I have an envelope for each of you with a copy of the miscellaneous items list, plus a copy of his will that our lawyer prepared for each of you. If you have any questions, just call the lawyer. His name and number are in the paperwork. Do you have any questions?"

They paused. Each sister opened their envelope and glanced through the contents.

Marge broke the silence. "You're so organized, Demi. Thank you so much for that. How are you holding up?"

"Oh, I suppose about as well as can be expected, under the circumstances. You know, your father hadn't really been quite right for some time. I would say that I first started noticing it after we came back from our Mexico trip."

"Wow," Marge remarked. "That was three years ago."

"I had a sense he wasn't himself," Carol said. "He looked like he lost some weight since then. The color in his face changed, too. I just figured it's how he was aging."

"I don't doubt that you were on to something, Carol," responded Demi. "His doctors said his cancer had to be present long before he finally went in. It's impossible to say how long it had been developing."

"I have something to say," Joan chimed in. "I think his problem goes way back."

"What do you mean, dear?" Demi asked.

"The syphilis finally got him."

Her remark startled all.

"What are you talking about," Marge challenged her sister. "Do you even know what syphilis is?"

"I know it's a bad sex disease. You know how I know? It's in the records at Southern Colony. When Jimmy had a lawyer get our colony records."

"I'm confused," Marge said. "What do you mean? What does that have to do with Dad?"

Joan answered. "The records showed that when Dad made me go there in 1948, he told them my problems came from syphilis when I was born. He told them Mama had syphilis really bad, too. Jimmy thinks that's why Mama was sick for so long."

Carol jumped in. "No, no, no. Ma had melancholia because of Baby Daniel. You know that."

"I know she did," Joan shot back. "She had both. That and syphilis. Jimmy thinks Dad had syphilis a long time ago. Then he gave it to Mama. What's the word, ummmm, infected? That's why I had birth defects. That's why Mama was sick. Her body was sick and her mind was sick from syphilis."

Both Marge and Carol looked at Joan like she was talking gibberish.

Marge piped in. "Joan, I hate to say it, but Jimmy doesn't know what he's talking about."

Joan stood her ground. "Oh, yes he does. He has a record of it. I can show it to you."

"If that's true, why haven't you brought it up after all this time?" Marge asked.

"We were afraid to," said Joan.

Bewildered, Marge wondered aloud, "Afraid? Why would you be afraid?"

"We were afraid what Dad might do," Joan said, her voice cracking with emotion.

"Stop! Please, just stop, both of you," said Demi firmly, her voice raised uncharacteristically. She sighed and shook her head. "My, oh my. I expected this might come up some day, but not today." After a pause and a deep breath, she continued: "I know about some of this. I found out about ten years ago. Your father was being so difficult to live with; I threatened to leave him unless he straightened himself out. He broke down and told me. He told me everything."

"Told you what?" Carol asked, clearly upset. Her face reddened.

"Your father did have syphilis a long time ago. He didn't know it at the time, but he passed it to your mother, and yes, it affected Joan when she was born."

As Demi explained, she could see the shock in the faces of Carol and Marge.

"He didn't know it. Your mother didn't either. They found out when she was hospitalized years later. The year the twins were born. She was in late stage syphilis at that point. She knew it would probably take her life. Your father got tested. His syphilis went dormant. It didn't affect him. He was told it could come back or it never will. He was lucky."

"And that's why he had me tested. That's when he found out," Joan recalled.

"Now I remember," Carol said. Her voice was shaking. "We all got tested." She looked at Marge. "He took us to the hospital for a blood test, remember?"

"Of course," Marge said. "I was scared. I had never been to a hospital before. We went. It didn't take that long. He never talked about it after. Never understood what it was for."

Demi interjected. "He told you your mother died from a broken heart because your baby brother died, right? That's what he told me when he unburdened himself ten years ago."

Both Carol and Marge nodded.

"Did he tell you how she died?" Joan asked her stepmother.

"Yes, he told me not long after we first met. I understand she killed herself with his police gun."

"He could have done it. He could have shot her," Joan suggested.

"Oh, shut up!" Carol yelled. "How could you say that? My God, he wouldn't do that!"

"Jimmy said it was possible, too. Didn't it ever cross your mind, even a little?"

Carol replied, "He wouldn't have done that. My, God, that's crazy!"

"You see? That's exactly why I never said anything. I'm dumb Joan! I'm crazy Joan!" Rage propelled Joan to her feet. "Who's going to believe me? He said so himself, when he took me to Southern Colony. No one is going to believe *me*."

Joan sat back down and cried. Demi went to her and put her arm across her shoulders. While she comforted Joan, nothing was said until she stepped to her chair to sit back down.

"It crossed *my* mind," Marge said.

"See!" blurted Joan, looking at Carol.

"I'm just saying, it crossed my mind. It's not what I believe, but I thought it."

Carol shook her head. "Well, I haven't. Why would he do that to her, to us?" It wouldn't make any sense."

"Neither did Mom doing it to herself," Marge countered.

Demi jumped in. "Alright, please. That's enough. Here's what *I* have to say. Your father wasn't faithful. He used bad judgement, a long time ago. No question about it. I did at that age, too. His mistake caused terrible problems in your lives. If he did what you think he did, Joan, it was to end your mother's suffering. Do I think he would have done that? No. From what he told me about the past, I don't believe he ever really loved Ruth. I *do* believe he loved your mother very much. The best he knew how."

"Let's be honest," Marge said. "He had awful fights with Ruth. After she died, there were a few people in the neighborhood that wondered how he could have two wives that died."

"It happens," Demi explained. "It's not completely unheard of, someone losing two wives *or* two husbands. Believe me, I know how people will talk and assume the worst. Again, do I think your father would do such a thing? Of course not. I married the man. When I met him, he was handsome, he was charming, and he was funny. He was the most beautiful man I had ever met. I had no idea at the time that he was such a troubled soul."

They sat for a while in silence. Carol fought back tears. Four women emotionally drained. Four hearts forever in conflict over the man now departed.

Marge segued to something lighter and easier to swallow. "Are there any petit fours left?"

Demi replied "Ladies, as long as there are women like us, there will always be petit fours."

EPILOGUE

"All the world is a stage, and all the men and women merely players."
~Jaques, in William Shakespeare's As You Like It *(published in 1623)*

L ike the rest of us, not all of their lives went as they would have liked. My Beecher predecessors played their parts the best they knew how. This is their curtain call . . .

CAROL

My mother died in 1993 of complications following cancer treatment. She was 66. My father also died at 66, three-and-a-half years earlier after battling metastatic prostate cancer. She was lost without him. My life's sweetest heart was unassuming and smarter than she let on.

Through uncovering her past, her hidden strength is no longer hidden.

MARGE

Aunt Peg died in 2011 at 82. She spent over 10 years caring for husband Korty, who struggled with Alzheimer's disease until he died in 2008 at age 85. Peg and Korty. Beloved by family, neighbors, and friends more than any couple I've ever known. Fun-loving, infectious joy, always offering support and encouragement. *The* Beecher Matriarch. She was *The One*.

JIM

At age 56, Jim left the Beecher stage unexpectedly, suffering a fatal heart attack alone in his kitchen in 1994. A funny, gentle man who battled the bottle. After his stint in the Air Force, Marge took him in for several years, backed by unconditional support from husband Korty. Jim moved on to live in Brown Deer and worked for twenty years as traffic manager for a North Side manufacturing company. His friend Mary wanted to wed. They never did. Marge and Korty were his guardian angels to the end. His nickname for his sister-mother – *Maude*, the feminine name in German lore for one who *battles mightily*.

Uncle Jim and Aunt Peg – c. 1986

JOHN

Shortly after his father's death, John and his wife Diane suffered the tragic loss of their infant daughter to illness. For reasons unknown, they moved unexpectedly to an undisclosed location out-of-state. Years later, we heard they moved to Nebraska, where they raised two sons. This is my only picture of John, taken by Julie with me at his side during a mid-90's family reunion in Brown Deer Park. There I was, with a doppelganger of Milwaukee icon Reggie "The Crusher" Lisowski. Uncle John was as hilarious as I remembered from childhood. In 2007, he died in his sleep at age 69.

JOAN

With Jimmy, Joan had the love she always wanted from her father. They raised two daughters and a son, all born without their parents' developmental disabilities, something many didn't think was possible. When their nest emptied, they moved to Wisconsin Dells. Jimmy and Joanie made their place in the sun. Their marriage lasted 38 years, until Jimmy's death in 1997. He was 67. Joan died in 2005 at age 71. She was buried alongside Jimmy in Kenosha, Wisconsin.

Ward family photo − c. 1969
(courtesy of Jimmy and Kathy Ward)

DEMI

After her husband died in 1966, Demi auditioned for and landed the job of private cook for Ilma L. Vogel Uihlein, widow of Joseph E. Uihlein, former vice-president of the Joseph Schlitz Brewing Company and president of Second Ward Savings Bank. I occasionally visited Demi in her apartment above the limousine coach house on the grounds of the Uihlein Mansion on Lake Drive, where she lived until Mrs. Uihlein's death in 1983. Demi lived in a South Side apartment for two years before moving to live with her daughters in Kissimmee Florida. We exchanged letters until she literally couldn't write anymore. She died in 2000 and was buried in Rockdale, Wisconsin.

Me with Demi at Benihana's in downtown Milwaukee – c. 1987

BABY MARGARET

Fifty-two years after her birth and adoption, in 2010, the woman born as Baby Margaret applied at the Department of Children and Families in Madison to determine the identity of her birth parents. Armed with two names and the power of the internet, she contacted her three blood siblings in a matter of days.

In the fall of 2018, I met my "new" first cousin for lunch. Though I agreed to keep her identity confidential, I'm free to tell you she is a delightful woman, intelligent and perceptive. Her manner and humor felt very familiar.

When I asked what, if anything, she wanted me to say about her, it was this:

"As it relates to me and my blood siblings, it is important to point out the misconceptions of the era. Neither of our parent's developmental disabilities were genetic or something their kids could inherit, despite 'system' beliefs. I've heard some mention of a familial tendency to mental health issues. Hell, it seems these days almost everyone would raise their hand on that one."

My dear new cousin: as someone intrigued by studies on intergenerational trauma and the epigenetic origins of family pain, I'm over here on my branch of the Beecher Tree with my hand raised high.

A stealth cloud hung in the house of my youth. It trailed us, as anyone who has lived with one of my parents' seven children could tell you. We're a pleasant bunch of happy mask wearers with an underlying sadness. In psychobabble, it's called lyprophrenia. A vague remorse without cause that you can't explain, nor ever fully shake off.

MARIE

Since our return to Calvary in 2016, Julie and I could not find the slightest clue to why her grave went unmarked. We moved beyond questioning why, just as her five children surely did to move on with life. They carried her memory in their hearts. We've tried our best to honor her memory with a book and a stone.

After 80 years, her resting place is no longer anonymous. A beloved woman is buried here. Her name was Marie. She was our Grandmother.

www.ingramcontent.com/pod-product-compliance
Lightning Source LLC
Chambersburg PA
CBHW060008100426
42740CB00010B/1440